Against White Interiority

"Binkley offers a powerful critique of the emotional coping mechanism of white guilt that continues to paralyze well-meaning, often liberal, white people from actively resisting and dismantling structures of white supremacy. A very timely book."

—Brad Elliott Stone, *Loyola Marymount University, USA*

"Sam Binkley conducts an insightful, detailed, and timely analysis of how new racial sensibilities intertwined with the therapeutic ethos have become subtle forms of domination and constant (self-)surveillance under the banner of individual liberation and moral redemption. A must-read for anyone seeking a new and sensitive look to understand a complex phenomenon of great relevance and contemporary significance."

—Edgar Cabanas, *Universidad Autónoma de Madrid, Madrid, Spain*

"Against White Interiority offers a startling hypothesis: whiteness now demands self-scrutiny in order to question its implied privileges and racism, and such turn inward bears a striking analogy to the strict inner discipline therapy demands. These techniques of self-scrutiny do not transcend racism but are caught within its very logic. This disturbing and innovative thesis must be read and discussed by anyone interested in the analysis of the culture and politics of our time."

—Eva Illouz, Directrice d'Etudes, *EHESS, Paris*

Sam Binkley

Against White Interiority

A Racial Critique of Therapeutic Reason

palgrave
macmillan

Sam Binkley
Emerson College
Boston, MA, USA

ISBN 978-3-031-31827-6 ISBN 978-3-031-31828-3 (eBook)
https://doi.org/10.1007/978-3-031-31828-3

This Palgrave Macmillan imprint is published by the registered company Springer Nature Switzerland AG.
The registered company address is: Gewerbestrasse 11, 6330 Cham, Switzerland

For Jeff

Preface

This was a very difficult book to write, and I owe a tremendous debt of gratitude to those who provided an audience for my turmoil on this topic. This includes all those friends, colleagues and interlocutors who variously advised me to persevere, to proceed with caution or even to renounce entirely and abandon these musings on the new racial sensibility. All these voices added something to my understanding of what I was, and what I was not, trying to accomplish. I am grateful for my professional network at Emerson College and for the Huret Faculty Development Grant I received which enabled me to develop important elements of this book. I am grateful for the support of audiences and hosts for several academic talks given between 2016 and 2022, whose thoughtful feedback and commentary forced me to clarify my intervention and to concentrate my argument. I am doubly grateful to the editors and reviewers at Palgrave for leading me through the final stages of this project, and of course, as always to my wife Tomoko and my son Kai, for providing all the stuff that really matters. And finally, I dedicate this book to the memory of my friend Jeff Juris, who left us abruptly and much too early, taking with him his unique blend of wit and conviction that, over the too brief time of our friendship, consistently brought me back to myself.

Boston, MA, USA Sam Binkley

Contents

CHAPTER 1

White Secrets: An Uncomfortable Introduction

Abstract This introductory chapter provides a general overview of the book. It discusses the emergence of a "new racial sensibility" over the course of recent years, and considers the way in which this new sensibility imposes a therapeutic logic through an appeal to white interiority. It proposes that this sensibility might be assessed for its relevance to the wider project of anti-racism through the lens of what is described as an ambivalent critique. It is argued that while this new sensibility brings productive change to public culture, it also, in a subtle way, reproduces the white subjectivity it seeks to transform. It does this through a complex emotional pattern which involves shame and guilt.

Keywords New racial sensibility • Subjection • Shame • Guilt • Anti-racism • Ambivalent critique

This book tries to make sense of what I term the "new racial sensibility," and the forms of self-awareness this sensibility brings for those who identify as white. Following a series of events that began with the early #Blacklivesmatter demonstrations and culminated in the police murder of George Floyd in 2020 and the "summer of racial reckoning" that followed, this sensibility has brought about a shift in awareness around race, applying a powerful lens to the condition of whiteness, where whiteness is understood as both a global ideology with deep historical roots and an

S. Binkley, *Against White Interiority*,
https://doi.org/10.1007/978-3-031-31828-3_1

embodied way of being, a psychic constellation bound up with a deeply personal pattern of thought and feeling (Chang et al., 2020). Considered largely in the American context, this new sensibility locates whiteness somewhere between the grand sweep of history and the minutiae of everyday life. Drawing on enduring and subterranean conversations that have for a long time circulated through the folk-wisdoms and practical knowledges shared by people of color as they negotiate the precarity of the American racial order, the new racial sensibility espouses a white awakening—an invocation captured in the word "woke," whose original meaning designates a clandestine knowledge of the hidden threats posed by white racism to the dignity and integrity of black life. More recently, however, within the rhetorical style of the new racial sensibility, woke and the awareness it signifies has undergone a profound mutation, developing from a colloquial and fugitive usage into a formal, if speculative knowledge of whiteness as a moral and psychic condition. From its roots in vernacular knowledge, woke has grown in its prestige and influence, acquiring unprecedented institutional acceptance, even finding a space for itself among those many pedagogical and instructional discourses through which everyday conducts are regulated in contemporary life. Woke's power to draw out the hidden contents of white subjectivity has been incorporated into that pantheon of regulative rhetorics and special knowledges that, rooted in a uniquely contemporary therapeutic sensibility, offer advice and direction on the tasks, risks and challenges of modern life, exhorting white people to peer into their souls for evidence of the stirring of racial malice.

Through this new racial sensibility assumptions about white interiority are made. The everyday interactive styles that white people enact with friends and strangers, the patterned ignorances they maintain about other racial groups as well as assumptions around risk and security, the impartiality of institutions and their overall life chances—all these attitudes and outlooks are seen to express a unique inner condition that works to produce something much larger than the characterological foibles of white individuals themselves. White mental habits produce racialized public spaces and the indignities of racist interactions, but they also shape broad and global structures of racial inequality that extend from systemic economic dispossession to routine police violence, all under the rubric of a generalized "whiteness" (Frankenberg, 1993, 2001; Kendall, 2012). In this way, the private, psychic life of whiteness is confronted with the moral and political certainty once reserved for the critique of oppression on a more global scale. Through the lens of the new racial sensibility, the personal becomes structural, or, conversely, the structural is addressed through the qualities of the personal, and it is in this way that the new sensibility comes to operate through a set of conversations and practices that can be described as therapeutic. White people today are exhorted to turn their gazes inward and to take up the challenge of a unique white interiority with a sense of purpose and moral urgency once reserved for the critique of structural inequality itself (Kendi, 2019; DiAngelo, 2018). Moreover, it has been through this incorporation of a therapeutic sensibility that special knowledges about the white disposition have attained new levels of dogmatic certainty and self-confidence, internal coherence, institutional codification, and ultimately wide adoption across a varied range of governing discourses and practices. Just as today we are asked to govern ourselves liberally, mindfully, biopolitically and psychiatrically, to maximize our potentials, sustain positive outlooks, to control our body mass index and to express our most personal experiences in managerial jargons, so too in professional and personal life, in schools, workplaces and in public and intimate relations are we asked (or at least certain populations of white people are asked), to own our privilege, to call ourselves out, to make ourselves uncomfortable and to have difficult conversations, and in this way to govern ourselves racially—where racially means, in this context, introspectively. Such practices of therapeutic self-government require attention to submerged habits of privilege, casual though subtly motivated word choice, situated ignorances or the simple function of taking up space—all evidence of a foundational, underlying whiteness and a dependence on the subordination of others through long histories of racial violence (Ahmed, 2007). The incorporation of what had previously been dispersed and marginal ways of knowing into an integrated formation of government suggests that the new racial sensibility might legitimately be studied alongside those many subtle arrangements through which we are governed, and that give form and reason to our behaviors as expressions of an underlying psychic life (Foucault, 1991; Lemke, 2022; Dean, 1999).

As such, through the optic of the new racial sensibility, the critique of structural inequality is folded together with the ongoing excavation of a certain inner realm, a therapeutic secret. As in therapy, casual intonations give clues to hidden conflicts and latent traumas that lie dormant within. Mundane remarks are quickly read as symptoms of hidden fears and anguishes, traceable to a legacy of white supremacist violence that remains concealed, too heinous to show its face. Details are made to speak in a language that combines culpability with the cure. The condition of whiteness, where it is invoked as such, is a universally regrettable one marked by moral narcissism and childish self-delusion, a preference for banal escapism over the harsh realities of a parasitic dependence on those over whom one exercises unearned privilege. But whiteness's therapeutic secret is also a malady and a failing that one has to muster the will to confront, to work through and to take responsibility for on one's way to a healthier, more mature moral life. Such a whiteness is one that sits awkwardly between a psycho-somatic condition and a moral choice, between illness and a state of evil. It is a way of being that operates behind the backs of white actors, pulling the strings of everyday behaviors from the unseen folds of white racial habits that white people themselves lack the will to confront. Such whiteness is more than just a way of being: it is a chosen ignorance and a willful laziness, a passivity that surrenders to the docile pleasures of its condition, a malevolent cluelessness realized through inaction. Emergence from whiteness demands that we expose ourselves to the shocks of a rude awakening, that we rouse ourselves from this slumber. In this way, whiteness is wedded to a certain program: whiteness comes to us as an incomplete and obscure truth, a moral somnambulism that is at once veiled, yet which we are perpetually waking up to through the examination of our own everyday attitudes—the task of a certain uncomfortable self-inquiry for which techniques are proffered, supervision is sought and mentors are recruited. The pledge to "wake up from one's whiteness" implies, as Abram X. Kendi puts it, a certain commitment: "like fighting an addiction, being an antiracist requires persistent self-awareness, constant self-criticism, and regular self-examination" (Kendi, 2019, p. 23).

The new racial sensibility's governmental agenda derives from alignments it has formed over the course of its development from a racial survival strategy to a broadly disseminated managerial discourse and a penetrating therapeutic rationality. The critique of racial conduct is now folded together with a set of psychological and therapeutic conventions, and with all those techniques, expert knowledges, training methods and advisory literatures through which practices of self-inquiry and self-reflection are directed. In short, the new racial sensibility propagates a way of turning the subject in upon itself—a technology of subjection that shares key features with adjacent arrangements that variously make use of the prefix psy- (Rose, 1999; Burchell, 1996). It employs practices of individualization in which, as Mitchell Dean puts it: "individualism is not pure: it is something constructed with the help of experts and has an institutional face" (Dean, 2007, p. 67). Through the new racial sensibility, the invitation to examine one's whiteness assumes an imperative character that draws from long institutionalized tenets of organizational and educational psychology, life coaching, counseling psychology, self-help literatures, corporate wellness programs and the writings of therapeutic gurus (Rieff, 1966; Rimke, 2000; Rose, 1999; Illouz, 2008; Herman, 1995). Its exhortation to inwardness is undertaken in the name of a behavioral adjustment, a normalizing optimization operating in an indistinct zone that runs between the pathological and the immoral, between being and action. Inwardness is attained through the application of a certain therapeutic imperative, the need to overcome internalized resistances and denials, administered through a formalized protocol (Binkley, 2019).

To put things in this way may suggest that the new racial sensibility and the uncomfortable inwardness it espouses is here being subjected to a certain kind of critique: a suspicious reading, an exposé or a debunking. Readers may suspect that what's going on is a frontal assault, from either the right or the left, on all the things that this sensibility stands for, that the myth of white racism that this sensibility so aggressively promotes will be exposed as bogus, as entirely fictional. But this is not the kind of analysis that is being proposed. The reality of white racism is not questioned, nor are claims regarding the effectiveness of the new racial sensibility in disrupting destructive modes of white racial being contested in any simple way. This new sensibility, it is argued, as it appears in schools, workplaces and popular media, promotes a new civility, a new set of competencies, protocols and interactive norms that should be recognized and defended for their success in limiting intolerant behaviors and reshaping public life. Yet, at the same time and on another level, the effects of this new sensibility go beyond these purported objectives. While defending the new racial sensibility's democratic transformation of public life, I believe it is important to point out certain latent functions that this sensibility serves—functions that need to be examined and, in my view, challenged. The imperative of white inwardness, in subtle ways, hollows out those democratizing effects, while surreptitiously reproducing key elements of white racism through the very formal and technical character through which it does its work.

To put this differently, in what follows, the case will be made that it is possible to separate out the new racial sensibility's private and public effects, to support the latter while raising critical questions about the former. As a set of protocols for interactions with others, as a set of public conversations on the restructuring of institutions, the recognition of historical events, the cultivation of interpersonal competencies, the allocation of resources and the forging of new political wills, this sensibility brings a much needed shift in the way racial publicity is enacted. At the same time, as a guide for the renovation of white subjectivity through the cure of the white soul, even when practiced in earnest, the new racial sensibility does something very different. I will claim that it sustains and reproduces dangerous and harmful aspects of the subjective life of whiteness which support, in the long term, toxic features of the racial order itself—a function it accomplishes through the unique invocation of what I term a white interiority that serves the ultimately conservative function of preserving and reproducing key elements of white racism and with it the structures of inequality upon which white racism depends. In short, this book presents an inquiry into the assumptions and processes, arguments but also the patterns of feeling and affect that give reason to the new racial sensibility and its appeal to a great white interiority, for it is through this reason that this sensibility attains its dual function of both undermining while sustaining the racial order itself.

1 Interiority and the Racial Dispositif

This volume assesses the new racial sensibility in its capacity as what Michel Foucault termed a *dispositif* (though which I will occasionally refer to simply as a function, an arrangement, an effect or an apparatus). This word has a special place in the critical vocabulary of Foucauldian thought, the breadth of which my use here does not fully encompass. By dispositif I intend the following meaning: an arrangement of discourses, managerial rubrics, codified institutional practices, special knowledges, expert persons, canonical and minor texts, technical writings, field-specific vocabularies and felt urgencies centered on the need to address and regulate forms of behavior by inducing unique practices of inward reflection. What I like about this word, and what makes it so helpful to the analysis that follows is the plurality, and hence the ambivalence that it permits: the dispositif is diverse and dynamic in its operation, drawing on multiple and heterogeneous sources, while imposing effects on people and on their experiences that do not reduce to a single axis of power, a line or a trajectory (Foucault, 2003, p. 27). Because it composes so many elements and operates on so many distinct levels, it is possible to approach the dispositif with the attitude of a certain ambivalence. The dispositif of the new racial sensibility operates precisely on such separate registers. It challenges deeply entrenched habits of racial inequality and manifests new political forms, while at the same time it induces a certain form of reflection, a need to confront, capture, tease out and transform the obscure force of an elusive white racism that operates within the self and is the object of a new technology of inward study. There is a profound sense in which this psychologizing reflection functions as a dispositif, in the Foucauldian sense. It renders white interiority a sustained and ongoing question whose function is ultimately to reproduce the white racial subject as an ever-unfolding problem-to-be-resolved, an enigma to be perpetually opened up, overcome through reflection and self-inquiry. Our whiteness gives us the truth of ourselves, we are told, though it always withholds some final inaccessible element, the terminal secret of white being which remains perpetually beyond our comprehension. In this way, the program of white inwardness is administered in such a way as to both challenge white racism while also sustaining and conserving those effects of white racial subjection that make white racism possible. Even as the new racial sensibility interrupts the racialization of public space and the interactive conventions that inscribe racial civilities, it also preserves the white subject as the ongoing problem of a certain racial interiority and as an enduring racial secret. In other words, the problem of white interiority comes to function as a kind of sphynx, a hidden truth which pins us to ourselves, arresting our movements and tangling us up. It does this in much the same way that sexuality might have done in the texts of nineteenth-century sexologists, police and jurists—an effect which Foucault captures in relation to another important domain of subjective life: "What is peculiar to modern societies, in fact, is not that they consigned sex to a shadow existence, but that they dedicated themselves to speaking of it *ad infinitum*, while exploiting it as *the* secret" (Foucault, 1984, p. 35).

In what follows, the production of this white subject and the pinning effect of this interiority will be considered through a study of the new racial sensibility. Toward this end, two contrasting traditions will be employed which, in spite of their differences, fold into each other provocatively. The first, as we have seen, derives from Foucault and his critical genealogy of the psychological dispositif, which produces *homo psychologicus*—the inwardly oriented man of psychology whose regulation Foucault considers in the first volume of the *History of Sexuality*, particularly as it takes shape around the problem of sexual repression (Foucault, 1984). The second interprets this same production through a very different tack, interpreting those same effects of interiority and subjection from the perspective of the feelings that they induce—feelings, I argue, that are centered around shame, and the need to suppress or conceal shame behind responses of guilt (Leys, 2007; Sedgwick & Frank, 1995; Tomkins, 1962). Through the work of a certain theoretical labor, and with some degree of license, it is my contention that a Foucauldian analysis of the subjectifying effects of the dispositif can be fruitfully undertaken in a manner that departs from Foucault's strong emphasis on the discursive and institutional effects of power. It is possible to recast processes of subjection and interiority that Foucault assesses largely through a discursive lens, as relations of feeling, corporality and embodiment linked to shame responses, and to examine the ways in which these relations figure in processes of white racialization itself. In a sense, then, this analysis attempts to engage recent criticisms of Foucault from authors invested in affective and materialist properties of power, while retaining important elements of Foucault's analytic approach. Karen Barad, for example argues that Foucault fails to manifest what she describes as a "post-humanist understanding of discursive practices" (Barad, 2007, p. 148), blinding him to "the relationship between discursive practices and material phenomena; a dynamic and agential conception of materiality that takes account of the materialization of all bodies" (200). Similarly for proponents of affect, such as Nigel Thrift, Foucault's "attachment to discourse" is cited as the reason for his silence on affect and emotion (Thrift, 2007, p. 54; Wetherell, 2013). In spite of their many important differences, these two frameworks, I contend, overlap and reinforce each other in critical and important ways. Discourse and affect, institutional subjection and feelings of shame, mirror a dual rationality which, on the question of the subject of whiteness and its interiorities, trace a common rationality.

On the level of the dispositif, the program of white interiority can be understood to assume an operation not unlike that of the repressive hypothesis as related by Foucault in the first volume of his *History of Sexuality*—one that beckons a program, consolidated on all sides by discursive and institutionally sanctioned assumptions and methods. As Foucault states about sexuality, the effect of these operations is not necessarily to produce less racist subjects (any more than the incitement of the sexual subject to speech is aimed at producing less sexually repressed people), so much as to ensure that the labor of white racial introspection continues indefinitely, that the white subject remains permanently enmeshed in the activity of its own interrogation and self-regulation, and that any aberrant or deviant departure from this project is immediately collapsed back into that original program. Suspended in the endlessly unfolding work of her own self-decipherment, ever laboring on the hamster-wheel of self-disclosure, this subject continues to occupy the position of the racist, or the almost-not-racist—a racist always on the threshold of an emergence from her own racism. Interiorities, in this sense, do more than contain secrets: they pin us, devouring all our possibilities, presuming that everything can be boiled down to a singular, interior point of origin, an all explaining source. Interiorities ensure that whatever else happens, the great internal cause of our whiteness can explain and contain everything, and in this way, that nothing new will ever happen. To make this point, the discussion that follows attempts to describe the ways in which the new racial sensibility combines words and feelings, discourse and affect, to enact a certain institutional form through which a specific subjectivity is produced.

Through reflection on my own emotional responses to the new racial sensibility, as well as speculation on the emotions and attitudes of those around me who embrace this new sensibility in earnest, together with an immersive study of the literatures that compose the new racial sensibility read through the lens of a certain theoretical apparatus, I have come to understand the production of this subjectivity through a certain affective process not reducible to the forms of discourse. This process can be described as a dynamic effect, a to-and-fro emotional pattern whose movement expresses the production of this white subject, and whose trajectory will compose the focus of this study. To put it somewhat schematically, this pattern can be interpreted as the linked effects of, on the one hand, a disruption or a shock, and on the other a consolidation or a capture. White self-awareness induced by the new racial sensibility, it will be argued, opens a shocking, unsettling glimpse into a shadowy, frightening and mysterious white world, just as, at the same instant, this disruptive insight is captured, subdued and subordinated to a set of procedures, a proper technique and a normalizing order. The disruptive force of a sudden insight into oneself is quickly reduced under the effects of regulation: seized, mapped out, subsumed under a method prescribed by a technical operation. Self-encounter, as the shocking, vertiginous moment of a disturbing and uncanny glimpse into oneself, is, under the rationality of the new racial sensibility and the racial diagnosis, configured as a problem of interpretation and treatment, as the rumbling of an inner cause, a white interiority, a domain already mapped onto a professional grid known to the experts, its possibilities already incorporated into a foregone and fated operation, inscribed with the certainty of an already-known program consolidated by a therapeutic technique. The shock of a disturbing uncertainty is captured as it is "interiorized," configured as the expression of an interior force, reduced to a point on the topography of an unfolding white inside. The invocations and practices of white self-study that have recently become so prominent within schools, workplaces, activist networks, corporate retreats and reading groups, that proliferate in online culture and that have generated such a vast publishing genre centered on the need to induce white inwardness—these practices converge to produce such a double movement that both shocks and captures, inducing a strange self-awareness but also subordinating this awareness under the rubric of an inwardness, and in so doing ultimately sustaining this subject within the equilibrium of a certain racial order, a whiteness conceived through the permanent posture of a self unravelling that is never complete. Tracing the effects of this double movement constitutes the first and primary analytical project to which this study is committed—an analysis of the latent operation and the double movement of the new racial sensibility as a dispositif.

However, alongside and through this very Foucauldian framing is another engagement that traces this same doubling movement of racial interiority through a different lens, one that adds a very different texture to the conversation than one might expect from a straightforwardly Foucauldian read. This comes from a consideration of shame effects of white racial subjection, and from a perspective on subjection that draws on a contemporary conversation within what has been called shame studies. Recent reflections on shame have come from a variety of conversations extending across the humanities and social sciences, affect theory, critical theory, women's studies, psychoanalysis, queer theory, studies of incarceration and corrections, education and in recent debates in Holocaust studies. Within these conversations, the traditional view of shame as an ethically benign and politically harmful emotion has been challenged by assertions of shame's critical and generative potentials (Munt, 2008; Berlant, 2013; Sedgwick, 2003; Sedgwick & Frank, 1995; Tomkins, 1962; Agamben, 1999; Leys, 2007; Pattison, 2000; Tyler, 2020). The specific manifestation of white shame that operates at the heart of this double movement must be understood in this light.

The shame that I sense lurking within the new racial sensibility and that clings to these formations of white interiority is of a special nature, surpassing as it does the shame or guilt that white people might feel for their racist actions. It pertains to a more satiating shame, a shame not just for one's privilege or one's hidden racism, but for white racial being itself, and for one's very embodiment as white. Those shames, ontological shames, which result from the shock of a certain traumatic self-discovery, are important for the unique sense of social and affective productivity they imply. Such ontological shames make us view ourselves through the lens of a sudden traumatic estrangement that creeps up on and clobbers us from behind. But in the course of the shock they deliver, this white shame expresses a unique potential, an opening onto the possibility of making something new, of reshaping social fields, of imagining new subjectivities and of extending to others in ways that cannot be reduced to the traditional economies of recognition and identity, obligation and debt. Shame, through the shock it brings, is described here as a generative emotion, an "autotelic" affect that ricochets around the room like a stray bullet, seeking out new goals and objects, multiple in its direction and radically mobile in its attachments (Sedgwick, 2003, p. 19). White shame, as I intend the term, and the self-confrontation it induces, expresses such a generative potential, which includes the possibility of disrupting that cycle of reproduction through which the white subject remains pinned to its whiteness, and the racial order sustains a certain inevitability and equilibrium. As such, this discussion will call upon recent revisions of shame which have sought to redeem shame as a dynamic, affective response whose social productivity (that is, whose capacity to generate new relationships and new subjectivities, and thus to more broadly reimagine the racial field) goes beyond the purely reactive or narcissistic qualities with which shame is often identified (Halperin & Trauss, 2010; Harris-Perry, 2013; Probyn, 2005).

But there is another side to this process. As a study of the white racial dispositif will attempt to show, the productivity and inventiveness of white shame is intolerable to the apparatus itself, and to the new racial sensibilities through which the apparatus operates. Shame, which introduces instability and aberrant social productivities and whose mutations cannot be accurately predicted or integrated into the flow of a managed, racial sociability, must be constrained, normalized and channeled into predictable forms. Shame's productive shock, as we shall see, is captured: "called out" through acts of knowledge, its truth coerced into public view (even while some truth is always maintained in reserve). Shame, in order that it might be contained, must be transposed or reexperienced as a different emotion: not as shame, but as guilt. Guilt is what the new racial sensibility enacts, converting shame's shock into guilt's self-reflection and dutiful commitment. Guilt is the capturing moment of the dispositif to which shame's shock must submit. It is the normalizing effect in which not only the ontological confusion and the panic, but also the social productivity and inventiveness that follow from shame's shock are subsumed, remade as responsibilities and as expressions of culpability for what is going on in a sunken, interior white place. The transmutation of unstable, wily and productive white shame into the durable and measured norms of white guilt is the work, the therapeutic but also juridical task to which the new racial sensibility commits itself as it seeks to preserve its monopoly on racial affect, and to insulate white subjectivity and the racial order itself from any untoward shocks. It is through the work of this capture that a certain racial equilibrium is sustained, through which subjects are pinned and that whiteness remains white. In this sense, I shall argue, this transmutation of shame into guilt is a process that runs co-extensively with the technical field of white interiority itself, and with the decipherment of the white secrets thought to reside within. Interiority, in short, is the device of this capture. It is what white subjects feel guilty about, and as such, what pins white people to themselves.

As both a discursive and an affective process, the new racial sensibility undertakes precisely this double operation. Confronting the white subject with her own whiteness, the new racial sensibility interrupts whiteness's self-comfort through the strange encounter it induces, initiating a traumatizing and vertiginous sense of a certain inner mystery: "what am I?", while at the same time resolving this mystery through the rubric of a normalizing finality and a judgment: "what have I done? Who have I harmed and what do I owe?" Pivoting gingerly between the themes of an ontological question (shame) and a pattern of moral action (guilt), the new racial sensibility portrays whiteness alternately as a state of being and a pattern of conduct, as a sickness and a pathology, a dark secret and an enigma resolvable through a program of managed introspection, but also a retractable moral choice for which one bears responsibility. There is a sense in which all of this conspires in a certain operation of therapeutic governance that I will term managerial. Like therapists, managers want to restore us to who we are. They want us to stay the same, to show up for work at the same times, in the same clothes, and to interact with each other in predictable ways within the boundaries of a stable institutional equilibrium. The white racial subject who abandons herself in shock only to return to herself in guilt is a subject in the perpetual activity of self-management: an ongoing transformation that never actually produces anything new, whose effect is precisely to validate the activity itself without reforming the conditions under which it was undertaken. Like Alice in the Red Queen's race running always in one spot, the subject of the new racial sensibility has attained a certain managerial symbiosis: it is suspended in a permanent and sustained labor that preserves all the operations within which it is enfolded without disrupting the delicate latticework of racial sociability itself.

To conclude this somewhat reductively, the argument of this book can be stated: the new racial sensibility does many things, some of them quite valuable. It imparts pedagogies of public conduct that reform institutions and spaces; it brings together protest voices, demands for structural reform, for the transformation of institutions, for the reduction of everyday violence. But also, as it assumes certain therapeutic and managerial rationalities, this sensibility preserves important features of those racial structures themselves. It does this by quietly reproducing those modes of white racial subjectivity that perpetuate those structures and compound their effects. To make this claim is not to argue that one of these functions outstrips the other, that one is the mask and the other the truth, nor that they tally, in some way, as to render some ultimate assessment. Neither is it to claim that the most important problem with the existing racial order is the effect it brings to the subjective lives of white people. Such a claim would distract from the fact of black suffering that should remain central in any assessment of the American racial order. The aim of this book is to argue that the subjective lives of white people serve an important function through which racial structures are sustained and through which racial violences, however subtle and indistinct, are promulgated. A critique of those racial structures through which black suffering is normalized would do well to consider all the elements that contribute to the reproduction of the racial order, which include material and symbolic violences structured into our everyday lives, but also those subjectivizing effects, those institutional routines, vocabularies, techniques and methods through which subjectivities are produced, and through which modes of whiteness or inwardness are inscribed.

Foucault, I argue, gives us the tools to do that. Foucault describes the movement from a self-encounter to its incorporation, from shock to capture, as a form of regulated interiority. A transcription of this process onto the field of white racial affect traces this same double movement in the series that leads from shame to guilt. Indeed, guilt (where guilt implies the responsibility we have to repair our inner psychic abnormalities) plays a large part in this story, and in my assessment it is the conversion of shame into guilt which operates in the new racial sensibility and which gives it the function of an apparatus. I believe it is possible to study the reproduction of white subjection by drawing together elements from a broad range of fields: psychoanalytic, philosophical and sociological literatures on shame, which can be used to describe those mechanisms by which the shock of shame is induced, but also recuperated as the rumblings of a guilty white interiority.

This argument unfolds through five chapters. Following this introduction, the second chapter of this book, "The New Racial Sensibility," describes the social, historical and empirical context through which a new discourse of white self-examination is shaped. Tracing the largely American emergence of a critical discourse on whiteness over the past 20 years culminating in the summer following the death of George Floyd, a convergence of activist, therapeutic and managerial literatures is considered for the way it shapes a new imperative centered on white self-examination. A textual interpretation of this imperative, captured in a set of hybrid conversations that span social media, social justice self-help, autobiographical memoir, activist how-to literatures and other genres, all sustain a recurring engagement with the realm of white interiority and its secrets as a problem of self-government. A discussion of these literatures provides an empirical backdrop to other more critical arguments that appear in the following chapters.

The third chapter of this study, "White Shame and Racial Abandonment," shifts the focus from the discursive regulation of white interiority to the affective and somatic dynamics of this process, and specifically to the feelings of shame that define this new sense of whiteness. The relationship between race and shame is explored with specific attention to those moments of white fragility or white panic so widely documented in the literature of the new racial sensibility that occur as white subjects are confronted with the shock of their own racial being (DiAngelo, 2018). However, in place of a view of white panic as an expression of lapsed responsibility for racial domination, the case is made that such panics are rooted in a state of white racial being, and a specific traumatic self-encounter with this being in which, for a moment, whiteness itself appears strange and alien, but also pliable and new. This moment is of a more material character, embedded in effects of corporeal exposure already implied by the very concept of race itself. A reflection on the blush and its relationship to the raced body draws out the fleshy dimensions of this moment of white racialization and its attendant shocks and panics, but also proposes ways in which shame might be understood productively as an affective moment that opens new possibilities and new mappings of the racial field, specifically through the instabilities that it introduces. Moments of white shame, it is argued, compose a certain unhinging of the white racial subject, a shock, but also an openness to the Other, and a concrete sense of a shared social space.

With the dynamic specificity of white racial shame established, the fourth chapter, "Guilt's Capture," turns to the regulative function imposed through the new racial sensibility as the unstable subject of shameful white panic is consumed and reduced, absorbed back into an interior field where shame is reexperienced as guilt. Drawing from sociological literature on shame and social order, and from psychoanalytic insights into the need to bypass the traumatic content of shame, the transmutation of shame's self-disturbance into guilt's other-oriented inner quest is proposed as a means by which shame is avoided, concealed or withdrawn from a dynamic relation with the Other, but also redirected as it is consigned to an underground existence (Scheff, 2014; Lewis, 1971). Indeed, this transmutation of shame into guilt composes a central function of the new racial sensibility and of the apparatus through which its effects are distributed. The reexperiencing of shamed panic as a guilty response to what is thought to be an unresolved inner condition, and a resolve to "do better" by assuming responsibility for one's internalized white privileges, is the effect of a capture that is secured by the new racial sensibility and its appeal to white interiority. The consequent effect of this interiority is the constraining of the productivity of this unstable encounter, mapping the effect of the subject back onto the grid of a therapeutic interiority.

2 Toward an Ambivalent Anti-Racism

This project is imagined as an anti-racist one, although it is not an anti-racism that sits comfortably with its time. The prefix "anti-" that affixes to the project of anti-racism, along with the invitation to join the author in being "against" white interiority, all suggest a critical style that draws clear lines, that knows what it likes and what it doesn't like and is in no mood to split hairs. However, the discussion that follows is marked by a more ambivalent sensibility than these dichotomizing expressions seem to suggest. In what remains of this introduction, I will try to convince the reader of the compatibility between the ambivalent tone of the present critique, which views the new racial sensibility multiply as both an asset and a hinderance in the struggle against racism, and the more strident commitments of an anti-racism that views white interiority as something that one should stand against. But this is already a difficult undertaking. Ambivalence, as the anthropologist Mary Douglas once wrote, stands in opposition to order in a manner not unlike dirt's opposition to cleanliness. Ordered systems of thought cannot tolerate those anomalous forms that resist quick reduction to the binary categories through which we organize our experiences and construct our worlds (Douglas, 1966, p. 5). Neither this nor that, ambivalent forms, like dirt, irk us, moving us to cleanse and to dichotomize, in an effort to reduce anxious ambivalence to a state of purity or cleanliness. In this sense, ambivalence and anti-racism make odd bedfellows.

I would hardly be the first to point out the sometimes hygienic sensibilities that permeate the new racial sensibility. Woke, some allege, is often marked by categorical rigidity and a relentless pursuit of orthodoxy. Like a religious system, woke is replete with its own roster of martyrs, blasphemies, cleaning rituals and pollution anxieties (Dean & Zamora, 2022). Former president Barak Obama put it this way in a much publicized interview in 2019: "This idea of purity and you're never compromised and you're always politically woke and all that stuff, you should get over that quickly. The world is messy. There are ambiguities" (Jabali, 2019). Similarly, popular authors such as John McWhorter or Greg Lukianoff and Jonathan Haidt have lamented the purity of cancel culture and the rigidity of contemporary "third wave anti-racism,"—criticisms that flow not from the pens of right-wing hacks but writers generally sympathetic with these movements themselves. By this token, it is fair to characterize the new racial sensibility by a certain stiffness, punctuated by what Robert Jay Lifton, in his classic studies of the ideological totalism of Maoist reeducation camps, identifies as "thought terminating cliches," slogans that suppress ambiguity through the imposition of clear moral distinctions. Such totalism, Lifton tells us, operates through a style of argumentation that is "prematurely abstract, highly categorical, relentlessly judging," that affirms tribal membership at the expense of critical reflection—a style characterized by the belief, as Lifton puts it: "'He talks like us' is equivalent to saying 'he is one of us'" (Lifton, 1963, p. 429). While such criticisms might justifiably be directed against the new racial sensibility, they should also take into account the context within which this sensibility was forged and the powerful challenges it faces. As one would expect of any grassroots political rhetoric emerging under the blows of a fierce political backlash (three years past the George Floyd demonstrations American schools and libraries are awash in demands for the banning of authors associated with "critical race theory"), it is not surprising that the new racial sensibility tends to display a general intolerance for ambiguity. Moral urgency requires a strategic language capable of addressing precarious times, and the new racial sensibility has met the demands of its moment with a proliferation of highly charged acronyms, vernacular and slang, quickly taken up on social media platforms and widely used in popular conversations and corporate jargon. Its purported rigidity is, in part, a response to these challenges. To point this out is not to diminish the political and historical importance of this sensibility, nor to attempt to explain away its critical contributions. It is to suggest that what is useful for political rhetoric might not be best for thinking, and thinking (particularly "dirty" thinking capable of maintaining ambiguous commitments) is essential to sustaining the political as an engagement with the diversity and ambiguity of human experience. Or, to put this differently, a critical ambiguity, while not reducible to political strategy, is nonetheless strategic in a broader sense.

Such an ambiguity seems a particularly timely asset as the new racial sensibility enjoys unprecedented levels of popularity and enters into institutional partnerships unheard of in the history of anti-racist discourse in America. Ambiguity is a way of countering the instrumentalization of anti-racism as a managerial tool, and of reclaiming the critique of whiteness as a place, not just for strategy but for social productivity, for the making of new political and subjective possibilities. At the same time, ambiguity, for it to remain critical, must mark its own limit: critical ambiguity is not a simple shrug in the face of choices that are too difficult to make, particularly where those choices involve our responses to the suffering of others. The critical ambiguity I propose is one that, while it seems to question some of the anti-racist left's most dramatic successes, does not lose sight of the human suffering that is at stake in any discussion of the American racial order. In fact, I would argue, those commitments remain central to the critical thrust of this book.

Readers will ultimately determine for themselves whether this volume suffices as an anti-racist text according to their own engagements with the racism they encounter. However, it is worth mentioning that, at least in the mind of its author, there is a sustained anti-racist thread that runs through this discussion, one that draws on a contention central to Foucault's critical sensibility, and specifically on Foucault's observations regarding the importance of subjectivity in the wider operation of power. For Foucault, the arrangements by which subjectivities are produced (a process in Foucauldian scholarship variously termed subjection, subjectivization or subjectification, although I will prefer the former term for reasons of accessibility), the institutions, texts, knowledges etcetera through which persons are drawn into urgent and practical relations with themselves, matter crucially in the reproduction of structural arrangements of power. Foucault tells us that structural practices or regimes of subjection (that is, those practices through which people are induced to become subjects, to examine and inquire into themselves in ways that ultimately produce themselves as certain kinds of individuals), whether medical, theological, educational, psychiatric, military, economic or biopolitical, serve essential functions in the reproduction of much larger orders, structures of coercion, domination and exploitation that might seem to have no direct link with subjectivity itself. All societies possess such regimes of subjection, nested into various institutional arrangements, social fabrics, structures and processes of power from which they serve as important nodal points in the reproduction of those structures themselves. But at the same time, Foucault pointed out, such regimes of subjection have also served as sites of contestation, often becoming the focus of unique and specific struggles. Foucault argued for the centrality of these regimes, as well as the critical potential bound up in these "struggles against subjection" for any wider critique of structural power:

> Generally, it can be said that there are three types of struggles: against forms of domination (ethnic, social and religious); against forms of exploitation that separate individuals from what they produce; or against that which ties the individual to himself and submits him to others in this way (struggles against subjection [*assujettisement*], against forms of subjectivity and submission).
>
> It is certain that the mechanisms of subjection cannot be studied outside their relation to the mechanisms of exploitation and domination. But they do not merely constitute the "terminal" of more fundamental mechanisms. They entertain complex relations with other forms. (Foucault, 1996, p. 331)

The religious strife brought by the European Reformation provides, for Foucault, an instance in which struggles have taken place over a disputed means of subjection as "that which ties the individual to himself and submits him to others," though he could easily have gone on to list several other such struggles that have appeared at various points in his work: the struggles of the mad against the psychiatric apparatus, of the sexual deviant against the bio-normative regulation of sexual life, etcetera. Indeed, his own remarks on political spirituality in Iran and the "desexualization" of bodies and pleasures in the S&M subcultures of San Francisco all point to the importance of political struggles centered on the need to contest the means by which subjectification processes are regulated and controlled, and relations of subjectivity are constrained within normalizing parameters.

Similarly, as we shall observe, the new racial sensibility, while fashioning new civilities, also exercises a latent and undeclared function in sustaining processes of white racial subjection, and hence, indirectly and in a subtle way, in the reproduction of the broader racial order within which whiteness finds a certain fit. As such, the interrogation of white subjection involves so much more than the unhappy lives of white people: it examines an important node within the larger reproduction of the structural order of white supremacy, one that perpetuates the harms and violences of the racial order itself. Such orders, after all, require more than just institutions, resources, symbols, economies, etcetera to keep themselves going. They also require subjectivities—technologies for being a self, for puzzling over, fearing for and attempting to get to the truth of that self. They require normalizing ways of conceiving and going to work on that self's possibilities and limitations and for seeking after that self's truths, both for those that are impacted by social violence and those that wield it. Thus, it is argued here that the decision to highlight white interiorities, white shame, white subjectivity etcetera is not a choice to elevate a concern for white psychic life over the harms done to others, nor to diminish the importance of more direct forms of violence that operate within this order. It is not to claim that all one now has to do as an anti-racist is to stay home and attend to one's own whiteness, or that such concerns should replace those more activist strategies proffered by the anti-racist left. It is to argue that a critical assessment of modes of white racial subjection provides an essential element in the broader critique of the structural ways in which racial suffering is normalized. White racial subjection, the fact of white subjectivity itself and the optic of a white interiority that it administers, composes a key feature of those systems that make such violences work. To inquire into those modes of white racial subjection that work in subtle ways both to challenge but also to consolidate the racial order, that upset its operation while naturalizing the sensibilities through which it operates, is in itself an anti-racist task. To make a critique of those modes of subjection is to level criticism, not simply against a certain set of bad institutions and bad actors, but against the multiple ways in which a certain heterogeneity of actors, discourses, affects and institutions operate in an odd consort, against the subtle and unseen effects that pass through constellations of good and bad actors, and against the subtle and indirect alignments to which such actors conform. And this means dropping the requirement that we be simply for or against things. It asks that we consider things in their multiplicity, through an ambivalent lens. Hence the necessity for a certain ambiguity, although, it is hoped, this is an ambiguity that doesn't lose track of what it means to be an anti-racist.

To state what should be obvious, it is nowhere suggested in this study that white subjects should be registered as dominated by these practices, nor that their feelings of shame or guilt are moral problems that deserve consideration as ends unto themselves independently of the structures of inequality with which they conjoin. In that sense, this study goes against a certain Foucauldian pattern, in which processes of subjection are typically depicted as overlapping with broader relations of domination, such as those imposed on gay men, Iranian students, itinerant peasants etcetera. The same cannot be said of those mechanisms of white subjection which work, conversely, to ensure only that the material domination of others proceeds smoothly. Readers who wish to read this essay as a weepy appeal to white victimhood, or who would employ this study to bolster a characterization of woke as a new authoritarianism will have to ignore, and even distort significant portions of this argument and the manner in which it attempts to apply Foucault's understanding of how power operates. At the same time, readers who might charge that this analysis is one that lets white folks off the hook too easily by placing white anxieties over the real suffering they cause, that it gives comfort to white racism by valorizing a posture of shame, or that it fails to manifest sufficiently militant opposition to white supremacy, should not forget Foucault's plea that practices of subjection play significantly in the reproduction of those relations, and that a critique of those practices of subjection plays a strategic role in an attack on structures of oppression themselves. What is at stake here is not a sovereign moral choice of white tyranny, nor an order that tyrannizes whites, but a complex set of relations that produces a mode of subjection embedded within the wider structure of a new racial sensibility that carries out the ambiguous function of reducing but also in a subtle way multiplying real suffering. A critique of those forms of white racial subjection, which "ties the individual to himself," as Foucault put it, is about much more than just the welfare of white subjects, about their well-being and bellyaching, their emotional lives and their feelings of comfort within a given arrangement. White subjectivities are important because they comprise a key element in the overall structure of the racial order, and the transformation of those subjectivities is a project with consequences that extend beyond the subjective lives of white people themselves.

The confrontation that this discussion imagines is not one that encounters problems head on, with the certainty of a strategic assault and along a bifurcated frontier of hardened positions. It is an ambiguous engagement that is negotiated laterally, from the side, along an angle that makes traditional dichotomies seem strange and conspicuous—an engagement that replicates what Foucault once said about his own method: "I am like the crawfish, I move sideways" (Foucault, 2008, p. 78). In a polarized environment and on a polarizing topic on which reading sensibilities are often shaped by a certain hygienic intolerance for dirt, I ask to be granted the space of such dirty ambivalence. I ask this with the humility of the crawfish, and with a full understanding that, in the present moment not everyone will be prepared to grant me this lateral movement.

References

Agamben, G. (1999). *Remnants of Auschwitz: The Witness and the Archive* (D. Heller-Roazen, Trans.). Zone Books.

Ahmed, S. (2007). A Phenomenology of Whiteness. *Feminist Theory, 8*(2), 149–168.

Barad, K. (2007). *Meeting the Universe Halfway: Quantum Physics and the Entanglement of Matter and Meaning*. Duke University Press.

Berlant, L. (2013). *Cruel Optimism*. Duke University Press.

Binkley, S. (2019). Unlearning Privilege: The Therapeutic Ethos and the Battle Within the White Self. In D. Nehring, O. Jacob Madsen, E. Cabanas, C. Mills & D. Kerrigan(Eds.), *The Routledge Handbook of Global Therapeutic Cultures*. Routledge.

Burchell, G. (1996). Liberal Government and Techniques of the Self. In A. Barry, T. Osborne, & N. Rose (Eds.), *Foucault and Political Reason*. UCL Press.

Chang, A., Martin, R., & Marrapodi, E. (2020). Summer of Racial Reckoning. Podcast. Retrieved June 12, 2023 from: https://www.npr.org/2020/08/16/902179773/summer-of-racial-reckoning-the-match-lit

Dean, M. (1999). *Governmentality: Power and Rule in Modern Society*. Sage.

Dean, M. (2007). *Governing Societies: Political Perspectives on Domestic and International Rule*. Open University Press.

Dean, M., & Zamora, D. (2022, August). Politics as a Confession: Confronting the Enemy Within. *Political Theology, 24*, 1–16.

DiAngelo, R. (2018). *White Fragility: Why It's So Hard For White People To Talk About Racism*. Beacon Press.

Douglas, M. (1966). *Purity and Danger*. Routledge.

Foucault, M. (1984). *The History of Sexuality, Volume 1, An Introduction* (R. Hurley, Trans.). Vintage Books.

Foucault, M. (1991). Governmentality. In G. Burchell, C. Gordon, & P. Miller (eds.), *The Foucault Effect: Studies in Governmentality* (pp. 87–104), translated by Rosi Braidotti and revised by Colin Gordon. University of Chicago Press.

Foucault, M. (1996). The Subject and Power. In James D. Faubion (ed.), *Michel Foucault: Power* (R. Hurley & Others, Trans.). The New Press.

Foucault, M. (2003). *Society Must be Defended: Lectures at the Collège de France, 1975–76* (D. Macey, Trans.). Picador

Foucault, M. (2008). *The Birth of Biopolitics: Lectures at the Collège de France, 1978–1979*. (G. Burchell, Trans.) Picador

Frankenberg, R. (1993). *White Women, Race Matters: The Social Construction of Whiteness*. University of Minnesota Press.

Frankenberg, R. (2001). The Mirage of an Unmarked Whiteness. In B. Brander Rasmussen, E. Klinenberg, I. Nexica, & M. Wray (Eds.), *The Making and Unmaking of Whiteness*. Duke University Press.

Halperin, D., & Trauss, V. (Eds.). (2010). *Gay Shame*. University of Chicago Press.

Harris-Perry, M. (2013). *Sister Citizen: Shame, Stereotypes and Black Women in America*. Yale University Press.

Herman, E. (1995). *The Romance of American Psychology: Political Culture in the Age of Experts*. University of California Press.

Illouz, E. (2008). *Saving the Modern Soul: Therapy, Emotions, and the Culture of Self-Help*. University of California Press.

Jabali, M. (2019). Barack Obama Thinks 'Woke' Kids Want Purity. They Don't: They Want Progress. *Guardian*. Retrieved June 12, 2023 from: https://www.theguardian.com/commentisfree/2019/nov/01/does-obamas-critique-of-radical-politics-help-bring-about-the-change-he-wanted

Kendall, F. (2012). *Understanding White Privilege*. Routledge.

Kendi, I. X. (2019). *How to be an Antiracist*. One World.

Lemke, T. (2022). *Foucault's Analysis of Modern Governmentality: A Critique of Political Reason* (E. Butler, Trans.). Verso Press.

Lewis, H. B. (1971, Fall). Shame and Guilt in Neurosis. *Psychoanalytic Review*, 58 (3).

Leys, R. (2007). *From Guilt to Shame: Auschwitz and After*. Princeton University Press.

Lifton, R. J. (1963). *Thought Reform and the Psychology of Totalism: A Study of "Brainwashing" in China*. Norton.
Munt, S. R. (2008). *Queer Attachments: The Cultural Politics of Shame*. Routledge
Pattison, S. (2000). *Shame: Theory, Therapy, Theology*. Cambridge University Press.
Probyn, E. (2005). *Blush: Faces of Shame*. University of Minnesota Press.
Rieff, P. (1966). *Triumph of the Therapeutic: Uses of Faith After Freud*. University of Chicago Press.
Rimke, H. M. (2000). Governing Citizens Through Self-Help Literature. *Cultural Studies, 14*(1), 61–78.
Rose, N. (1999). *Governing the Soul: The Shaping of the Private Self*. 2nd edition. Routledge.
Scheff, T. (2014). The Ubiquity of Hidden Shame in Modernity. *Cultural Sociology, 8*(2), 129–141.
Sedgwick, E. K. (2003). *Touching Feeling: Affect, Pedagogy, Performativity*. Duke University Press.
Sedgwick, E. K., & Frank, A. (1995). Shame in the Cybernetic Fold: Reading Silvan Tomkins. In E. K. Sedgwick & A. Frank (Eds.), *Shame and its Sisters: A Silvan Tomkins Reader*. Duke University Press.
Thrift, N. (2004). Intensities of Feeling: Towards A Spatial Politics of Affect. *Geografiska Annaler: Series B, Human Geography, 86*, 57–78.
Tomkins, S. (1962). *Affect, Imagery, Consciousness* (Vol. 4). Springer.
Tyler, I. (2020). *The Machinery of Inequality*. Zed Books.
Wetherell, M. (2013). Affect and Discourse—What's the Problem? From Affect as Excess to Affective/Discursive Practice. *Subjectivity, 6*(4), 349–368.

CHAPTER 2

The New Racial Sensibility

Abstract In this chapter, the premise established in the introductory chapter is developed and elaborated. The new racial sensibility is described as a popular cultural form which expresses a specific relationship to textual and verbal expression. The therapeutic appeal to white interiority that it pursues is read in relation to wider emotional patterns which disrupt the white subject through experiences of shame. In response to such a disruption, the textual form of the new racial sensibility imposes narrative and discursive coherence through a discourse on white interiority intended to offset shame's disruptive effects. Moreover, this wider tendency is read through Michel Foucault's theory of subjection, translated from a field of discourse to one of affect, specifically shame and guilt.

Keywords Shame • Guilt • Woke • Discourse • Foucault • Subjection

Recent years have witnessed a concerted challenge to the cultural authority of whiteness. In the United States, prompted by a series of highly publicized police murders and other events, a new public discussion on race has spread from social media enclaves and activist circles into the popular conversation. The election of the nation's first African American president, the murders of Freddie Gray and Trayvon Martin, demonstrations in Ferguson and other cities and the emergence of the #Blacklivesmatter movement trace the gradual growth of a critical attitude that has intensified over the years, culminating in protests following the killing of George

S. Binkley, *Against White Interiority*,
https://doi.org/10.1007/978-3-031-31828-3_2

Floyd in the summer of 2020 and bringing a new awareness of the racial sentiments that underpin public life. What I term the new racial sensibility bridges the spectacular and the mundane: public gestures of dissent from high-profile figures in sports and entertainment resonate with an emerging awareness of the subtle presence of racism in routine encounters and everyday utterances. As such, this new sensibility is not entirely new: awareness of such racial undercurrents has become increasingly central to the self-understandings of American middle-class whites since the 1960s, although, as is frequently argued, this awareness is often stifled and obstructed through a variety of obfuscating tactics (Balibar, 2011). White racism, it is widely acknowledged, operates in a zone of affect and thought that is hidden from casual view (Ahmed, 2007; Alcoff, 1999, 2015). Behind the veneer of white civility one detects latent, unseen and benign formations of racial anxiety, particularly in the attitudes of those who outwardly espouse a non-racist politics (Sullivan, 2006, 2015).

What is new about the new racial sensibility is not only the breadth of its adoption across a range of institutional settings, management practices and public policy debates from policing to housing to media representation, but also the extent of its penetration into the very textures of everyday social life. Critics point to the mushrooming scale of the diversity, equity and inclusion (DEI) industry, which in 2020 was estimated at 7.5 billion dollars a year—a figure which, given the pace and trajectory of industry growth, is expected to grow to 15.4 billion dollars by 2026 (Global Industry Analysts, 2021). Among its many agendas, the new racial sensibility seeks to make conspicuous the deeply internalized attitudinal biases that characterize the contemporary racial order, calling upon white supporters and activists to commit themselves to an open-ended program of reflective self-inquiry. As a consequence, many white people in the United States today are increasingly inclined to embrace this call to ferret out unconscious attitudes folded into unseen emotional and somatic habits. The swift dissemination of a program of white interiority and its broad acceptance across a variety of (largely middle class, largely liberal) constituencies has led its supporters to hail a long overdue period of "racial reckoning" in a country that has long avoided any acknowledgment of the racial violence upon which it was founded (Chang et al., 2020). A wave of introspective pronouncements has prompted proponents to praise steps toward the long delayed dream of American racial equity, while detractors draw comparison with other American panics and hysterias from McCarthyism to the Great Awakening (Yglesias, 2019; McWhorter,

2017). As an abstract aspect that bypasses the intersectional specificity of any particular white identified population, white attributes emerge as "whiteness"—a reified element whose presence can be felt and whose movements can be anticipated. The imperative of a certain white introspection has left its mark on a range of institutional practices and protocols from education and business to government, popular culture and public life. White interiority, once a marginal problem confined to a remote convergence of activism and self-help, has today emerged as one of the primary domains of expertise through which public and private life is governed—so much so that it is possible to assess its influence the way we would other discourses and practices through which the regulation of attitudes and behaviors is carried out. Expert rhetorics on white racism rank among a plurality of regulative pedagogies and instructional conversations aimed at such problems as public health, domestic violence, hygiene, alcoholism, childrearing, genetic predisposition, career development, emotion management, neighborhood security, family planning, work-life balance, saving for retirement and myriad other areas of our lives that variously fall under the instruction and tutelage of the expert professions. Now our racism too is one such problem, the precise depth and character of which is known to a new cohort of race experts who imbue our lives with ordinances, rationalities and techniques. Because of its current ubiquity, this new governmental arrangement needs to be studied and understood.

The new racial sensibility composes a program of self-study centered on the excavation of an inner psychic trace, an unreconstructed racist attribute that operates often behind the backs of white subjects themselves. White racial self-monitoring has emerged as a hygienic competency, a sensitivity and a racial literacy to be cultivated in oneself and exposed where it is lacking in others, administered by institutional professionals and media experts who profess knowledge of the white soul and its tormented secrets. This sensibility enacts a certain feel for everyday life which might be described as hermeneutic in character: it involves the work of reading through the layers of one's own and other's racial defenses and obfuscations to tease out the latent movements of a recalcitrant white psyche. It directs us to a subtle play of signs in speech and behavior, sensitizing us to the undercurrent of a racism that evinces itself in the inflections of cadence, the furrowing of a brow, the choice of seating on public transportation or the trailing of a voice at the end of a sentence. Confronted with this new racial sensibility, some white constituents complain of feeling besieged, shaken under the force of a new and disturbing scrutiny. White people today not already invested in this project describe having to walk on egg-shells in public conversations, while those that embrace it describe an almost cathartic, anguished and long delayed moment of truth (Ahmed, 2012). Though responses vary, for many white people this awareness is only earned through an exercise that combines deft resolve, panic and humility. One must have the conviction and fortitude to confront one's internalized racism, in spite of the discomfort this brings and the unflattering image it portrays. Interiorities are always unsettling places to visit, and the program of white introspection issues a diffuse trauma and unique sense of dread at those specters of unacknowledged racial being that such an inquiry is likely to expose. Avoidance of such trauma leads many white people to shirk the challenge, and for this reason they require steadfast guidance. Indeed, trauma provides a certain validation of the introspective project itself: if we can learn to "sit with discomfort," it means the effort was at least undertaken in earnest.

The unsettling effects of this sensibility have descended unevenly. Typically blue state, liberal and coastal middle class, more apparent in the fields of education, human services and in the culture industries, the new racial sensibility is often ridiculed by its critics as a class-bound phenomenon—a liberal fad for "woke," or the latest trend taken up by the chattering, educated and coastal elites (McWhorter, 2021). Yet, it is my contention that this new sensibility, even where it is disparaged and mocked, has ignited a set of emotional responses within a variety of white identified demographics and populations. Whiteness, which once operated through its invisibility as an unmarked social and racial category is today made to stand out and to account for itself, made conspicuous to white people who are asked to recognize themselves for their long concealed racial particularity (Wise, 2010, 2011; Yancy, 2004; Dyer, 1988). In the wake of the #blacklivesmatter, #ocarssowhite and NFL protests, amid myriad media reports of racial violence, exposures of white racial fear and the everyday emotional labor that so many people of color now publicly describe, many white people find themselves, for the first time in their lives, directed to reflect on themselves through the lens of their own deeply internalized racial being, to take responsibility for the reproduction of this being and even to commit themselves to its transformation.

In the chapter that follows, I will engage this new racial sensibility and the program of white introspection it espouses through a discussion of the rationality through which it operates. Rationality in this sense implies the unique ways in which this sensibility makes sense of problems, attributes causes and applies solutions, but also mobilizes its own ways of knowing against these problems. Together these problems and knowledges compose what I term a program—a set of insights and knowledges, but also steps and actions to be taken up by individuals and applied to themselves and to others. The program of white interiority is not radically different from other agendas and conversations that are to be found embedded in our institutional and public lives, and that extend to the remotest realms of our private thoughts and anxieties. To be better spouses, we are told, we must delve into residual childhood memories, or to be better employees we must train ourselves to view work situations optimistically (Binkley, 2015, 2016, 2019a, 2019b). Such programmatic imperatives compose a subtle latticework of prompts and nudges that move us perpetually toward more intense forms of self-examination and self-work. In the case of the new racial sensibility, the argument will be made that such programs serve many constructive ends. They create new social habits and norms that reduce the strains of racial inequality. But at the same time, the charge will be made that these programs do not ultimately succeed in what they set out to accomplish, which is to transform the inner lives of white people. In fact, in specific ways, they achieve precisely the opposite: they confront this interiority under an implicit guarantee that key elements of the inner life of whiteness will remain stable and unchanged.

1 A White Awakening

The new racial sensibility combines a rich variety of historical and cultural influences and precedents (Lasch-Quinn, 2002). These not only include the contributions of activist networks, emergent managerial cultures and organizational psychologies, but also humanistic psychotherapies, elements of Western Marxism, Eastern mysticism, popular self-help and practical how-to literatures. All these influences are important, though in a general sense it is through an encounter with professional psychology that the new racial sensibility is made possible. Through a broad and uneven process originating with the successes and compromises of the civil rights movement in the 1960s and 1970s, a loose consensus was established that white attitudes had to be reformed in response to the presence of previously marginalized groups in public conversations, and that professional psychologies would lead the way in this process. White people would have to change—a task for which a new set of expert advice on the management and transformation of the human subject would be mobilized. Legislation regulating workplace compliance to title VII of the Civil Rights Act provides one scenario in which this new expertise began to take shape. With the rise of anti-discrimination litigation, a host of compliance-oriented, anti-bias training programs began to spring up in the 1970s, mostly restricted to the legal and managerial aspects of bias in hiring and promotion (Anand & Winters, 2008). By the late 1970s, however, the focus would expand to the personal and cultural climates of work environments themselves, and the need to adjust the social norms of professional life to include a more diverse population. In the American workplace of the 1980s, diversity and inclusion became not just a liability but an asset in attracting and retaining employees—a vision which opened a range of psychic and emotional domains to new forms of corporate management (Thomas & Ely, 1996). As diversity training programs became increasingly ingrained in professional cultures, a range of therapeutic methods were improvised, often patterned on humanistic and encounter group models popularized in the 1960s, and quickly replicated across a variety of fields from education to medicine, criminology, public policy and the family. In all these areas, white constituents were called upon to overcome their discomforts and resistances and to confront those unresolved racial anxieties that have for a long time shaped their outlooks and social identities.

The evolution of what we might term a technology of white anti-racist subjection can be traced through the implementation of a need to remake whiteness and its prejudices. With the publication in 1954 of Gordon Allport's *Nature of Prejudice*, white racism came to be understood as a pattern of flawed categorical thought, deeply embedded in the chauvinistic forms of everyday social typing among social groups (Allport, 1979; Cherry, 2000). Prejudice was conceived as a biased form of cognition in which appreciation of the subjectivity and the sufferings of others was distorted by pre-formed perceptions cultivated within the restricted memberships of one's own racial groups. Prejudice was "an antipathy based on faulty and inflexible generalization [which] may be directed toward a group as a whole, or toward an individual because he is a member of that group" (Allport, 1979, p. 9). However, within a few short decades, these patterns of flawed judgment would be transmuted into what today we call "unconscious bias," a configuration "...which encompasses both favorable and unfavorable assessments, [which] are activated involuntarily and without an individual's awareness or intentional control" (Kirwan Institute, 2012). In other words, over the course of a few years, the problem of white racism would acquire the character of a far more obscure and elusive abnormality of the cognitive and affective disposition—a "secret" capable of operating beneath the radar of individual consciousness, the identification, decipherment and correction of which would require ever more refined instruments and techniques. Over time, efforts at the transformation of this disposition would develop their own rhetorical form, employing narratives of self-transformation and renewal resembling those stories of self-renewal common in other popular self-help genres. "Why Some Whites are Waking Up to Racism," is the title of a 2016 *Washington Post* article, which recalls the words of white people from different walks of life striving for a new state of racial self-awareness: one woman describes the need to become "more aware of how unaware" she is; another says she is "looking for ways to dig into white privilege, to become more cognizant of it" (Schwartzman, 2016). In a memoir on white racial awakening titled *Waking Up White, and Finding Myself in the Story of Race*, Debby Irving gives words to this program: "when I was with a person of color, I felt an inexplicable tension and fear that I might say or do something offensive or embarrassing… Most confusing were unwanted racist thoughts that made me feel like a jerk… Learning about racism has settled inner conflicts and has allowing me to step out of my comfort zone with bold strength and vulnerability in all parts of my life." Yet, for Irving, this awakening is not one that comes with the grace of a sudden enlightenment: it is a gradual and active program to which she is committed:

> Waking up white has been an unexpected journey that's required me to dig back into childhood memories to recall when, how, and why I developed such distorted ideas about race, racism and the dominant culture in which I soaked. Like the memoir by the guy who loses two hundred pounds or the woman who overcomes alcohol addiction, my story of transformation is an intimate one. (Irving, 2014, p. 8)

Whites must do more than simply disavow distorted perceptual and cognitive habits, they must gather the will to confront unconscious biases. Whites must awaken themselves from their racial slumber and let the scales drop from their eyes, but to do this they must subdue long-held and deeply rooted habits of ignorance and denial, and learn to face themselves as they truly are (Metzl, 2019).

The fluidity and porousness which in recent years has enabled this sensibility to circulate so pervasively through such a plurality of institutions derives from its imbrication with what might be described as the *lingua franca* of governmental languages: the discourse of professional psychotherapy and the broader ethos of the therapeutic. White racial attitudes are today read through the lens of mental health, and treatments of racism as an attitudinal "condition" are modeled on a therapeutic process in which illness is resolved through the overcoming of deeply held resistances and habits of self-obfuscation. Indeed, whiteness and its recovery are understood by white people as a form of "work" comparable to therapeutic labor—a treatment that links personal and historical connotations to a narrative of civilizational progress, psychic development, moral maturity and medical cure (Katz, 1978). To be "back in the 1950s," or on the "wrong side of history" is to languish in a state of underdevelopment, to remain infantile or residual in the reconstruction of one's whiteness. This program tells a tale of moral, but also historical development in which generational frames are used to relate stories of relative progress: most white people consider themselves less racist than their parents or grandparents, but not as much so in relation to their children, who will have had more time to perform the work required for the transformation of their whiteness. Such a story was first told by Janet Helms, an early psychologist of the white condition who formed a developmental model of white reconstruction patterned on another popular trope, the "Negro-to-Black" model prescribed in the 1970s by black psychologist William Cross. Negro-to-Black traced a passage of psychological development leading from confusion and error to higher levels of self-actualization and overall mental health for black people. Through Helms' theory of white racial identity, a similar developmental process could be applied to whites, also described in incremental stages of enlightenment extending from the naïve state of initial contact with members of other races to the eventual attainment of a state of self-knowledge and self-acceptance as a non-racist white person (Cross, 1971; Helms, 1984, 1991). Both models see the moral process of overcoming racism as a problem of normal growth: racism is a state of pathological immaturity that is resolved through the gradual cultivation of a self-consciousness and a slowly manifested moral will, punctuated by unsettling and sometimes traumatic epiphanies. What is striking in Helms' version of this story, and the quality I wish to emphasize, is this folding together of therapeutic work with epistemological themes of an insight and special knowledge earned through trauma. These themes converge on a certain account of personal growth which encapsulates the need to sustain discomfort (and hence the necessity for labor) and the forms of knowledge derived from this earned insight. Moral and medical progress is attained through the overcoming of systemic ignorance. Those white people who are in need of such transformation are induced, through a set of exercises and appeals, difficult conversations and direct pedagogies, to take themselves and their apperceptions as the objects of a new sort of inquiry, one designed to lay bare long dormant and intentionally reticent attitudes and assumptions, secret pleasures and hidden anxieties that by their very nature escape detection.

An analysis of the therapeutic labor of white anti-racism is one that draws on an already well-developed tradition of research into those concentrations of expertise through which so many domains of personal and public life are taken as objects of government. Adjacent to his concept of the dispositif, Michel Foucault originated a term—governmentality—that has subsequently fostered an expansive field of research centered on a range of technologies, conversations, directives and exhortations through which individuals are urged to willfully direct their own conducts, to take themselves up as problems to be studied, interiorities to be probed, potentials to be maximized and abnormalities to be corrected (Foucault, 1991). Governmentality, a neologism combining the function of government with the rationality through which government is exercised, describes latent processes through which voluntarily assumed modes of conduct are made to appear practical, reasonable and urgent (Burchell, 1996). As such, this term has generated a diverse research agenda, directing Foucauldian inquiries into such realms as education, medicine, psychiatry and economic life—all those fields in which modes of human conduct are governed through the inscription of a certain practical agendas and techniques. In assorted advisory and pedagogical literatures, we are governed in the optimization of personal health, in the cultivation of career ambitions, in the performance of family responsibilities and in the seeking of romantic partners—myriad problems of everyday life whose critical ambiguity is absorbed into the practical problem of its enactment (Foucault, 1991; Rose, 1990, 1999; Dean, 1999). As Nikolas Rose puts it: "Thought becomes governmental to the extent that it becomes technical," aligning itself with those technologies through which specific modes of behavior are adopted and put into practice (Rose, 1999, p. 51). White racial interiority is the product of many things and forces, but most recently, it is the effect of the very arrangements of expertise and technical knowledge, the programs and mandates through which it is sought out and studied, worked through, woken up to, grown out of and made technical.

2 Governing the Racial Subject

To adapt Simone de Beauvoir's famous dictum: one is not born, but rather becomes a white racial subject. To state as much is not to say anything all that new: the literature on the social construction of racial identities has for a long time considered the role of culture and social membership in the making of racial subjectivities (Appiah, 1996; Goldberg, 1993; Zack, 2002; Mallon, 2004; Ignatiev, 1995). From the standpoint of historical, psychological and sociological critiques of white racism, the white racial experience is the indirect effect of silent processes of socialization and structural reproduction, shifting demographic patterns, implicit community norms, parenting practices, media effects and other diffuse and gradual influences through which in-group/out-group distinctions are formed and racial typologies are woven into everyday outlooks (Kovel, 1984; Bernasconi & Lott, 2000; Roediger, 1991; Fredrickson, 2002). But alongside this explanation, the silent "becoming" of the white racial subject might also be conceived as the intentional result of some very deliberate projects applied reflectively by the white subject to herself, such as those projects that derive from practices of self-government: pedagogies of professional and social life, instructional discourses on health, intimacy and social life, and psychologizing and therapeutic discourses on psychic and racial well-being. White subjects are made, but in many different ways, sometimes gradually and silently through patterns of family and community life, but sometimes loudly and with great fanfare, as the effect of direct purposes or doctrines of mental and psychiatric health (McWhorter, 2005, 2009).

In this way, the work of anti-racist subjection takes a curious form. As a racial project it implies an intentional reversal and revision, a peeling back and stripping away of some other already established, more settled and habitualized mode of white racial being. The chief instrument of this labor, I contend, is both doctrinal and epistemic: it is toward an acquired knowledge of what lurks beneath the social surfaces of the self that white subjects are exhorted, a project which signals an ongoing undoing and redoing of the racial subject. Indeed, what is described in the critical literature as a process of racialization can also be understood as a *de*racialization directed at the diminishment or removal of an unwanted residue of received racial attitudes and habits (Omi & Winant, 1994). Such a deracialization combines with what I will term a *re*racialization of the white subject—an intentional cultivation and production of new outlooks and sensibilities, new habits and new civilities. The white condition must be known and its secrets exposed, but to be known it must be undone and done again, and for this to happen one must unflinchingly confront the obstructions that whiteness puts up through the application of an intense mode of self-inquiry and self-monitoring. Such is the work that is bound up with the reracialization of white subjectivity: the production of a new self through the peeling back of masks to uncover and expose an underlying secret. In this way, reracialization implies a certain interiority that can only be accessed through the breaching of a concealing exterior: a sheltered and protected space constructed of obfuscating layers, which must be undone and penetrated in order that reconstructive labor might proceed.

These sentiments are captured in a workshop organized by an anti-racist group in Los Angeles in the summer of 2020: "Unmasking Whiteness." Promotional literature for the event provides a rationale for the group's focus: "To challenge racism, white people need to unlearn racism and discover how we enact white privilege. This is a long, difficult, and often painful process. Having a community of white anti-racist people gives us hope, helps us grow our practice, and gives us strength to stay in it for the long haul" (Aware, 2021). To undergo reracialization is, in this sense, to engage with a problem of exposure and self-study, but also to cultivate a certain fortitude and resolve necessary for a particular kind of ethical work. For the white racial subject, this means that whiteness itself must not only be coaxed into the light, studied, deciphered and condemned but also molded and reshaped into something new.

What we witness today, I think, is the embeddedness of a reracializing project within a style of thought and speech deeply imprinted by the medical and psychological professions, and by the therapeutic imperative itself, expanded here into a broad ethos, a therapeutic way of life (Binkley 2019a, 2019b; Lasch-Quinn, 2002; Gilman & Thomas, 2016). Viewed descriptively, the therapeutic ethos is one that employs a rationality and a logic that dislodges personal behaviors, relationships and life predicaments from any broader normative framework, assessing our behaviors as symptoms of underlying condition, comprehensible only in terms of our own formative psychic experience and history of emotional habits (Illouz, 2008; Sennett, 1976). Under this ethos, it doesn't matter if we are right or good. What matters is that we are authentic to ourselves and others. Where traditional notions of civil society and public conduct imposed a separation of public and private lives and allocated to public life certain forms of speech and conduct to be judged for the compliance with public norms, the therapeutic sensibility applies a diagnostic lens, reducing public performances to mere displays, layered maskings of private causes which must be read through the layered shell of outward appearance. A skilled therapeutic sensibility is one capable of reading everything in terms of its underlying emotional and psychic determinations. In so doing, the therapeutic ethos reshapes social and civic behavior along the lines of a medicalizing telos: speech and conduct are judged principally as a means of attaining psychological health or of deflecting psychological pain, and are in this sense taken as ends in themselves independently of any external validating scheme. The mere fact that one has "grown" or "expressed oneself," or that one is "harmed" or "made to feel unsafe," through a set of interactions is enough to validate or invalidate those actions on the basis of their therapeutic effect. As James Nolan writes, the therapeutic ethos, "unlike traditional moral orders, is at its heart self-referential" (Nolan, 1998, p. 2). Importantly, such self-referentiality is often guided by a belief in the medical and moral authority of the therapist herself. It is the therapist who leads the subject down the path of a painful but necessary self-confrontation through a pattern of carefully laid provocations and prompts. That one attributes to the therapist a certain authority to know and that one identifies with this epistemic authority allows the subject to assume a similar distance on her own psychic composition. As a social ethos, the belief that therapy opens a window onto an inner sanctum wherein a unique psychic turmoil plays out, and that one cannot open this window oneself but must call upon the superior knowledge of an expert, is central to the therapeutic project, giving form and reality to one's psychic difficulties while charting a path to an eventual cure. The attribution of such authority and the presumption of a certain omniscience thought to be possessed by a therapist who possesses the ability to see into the space of an interiority which the subject cannot see in her own self is central to the function of this therapeutic rationality, and composes a key operation of the new racial sensibility. In this way, the therapeutic ethos is antithetical to the public/private distinction that has long characterized Western thinking on the public sphere: the therapeutic gaze sees through the public performance to the underlying private conditions that animate public behaviors which are now judged on that basis, just as the therapeutic actor participates in public discourse through acts of self-exposure.

A short example demonstrates this therapeutic dynamic at work in the new racial sensibility: at a liberal arts College in the American Northeast, amid the demonstrations following the death of George Floyd, an email was sent to all students and faculty from an official charged with supporting the College in its diversity efforts.

> I am asking us now to do heart-work we may have never done before—the kind we may have avoided because of its potential to unsettle what we understand of the world, our communities, our cultures, and of ourselves. I am asking us to individually and collectively transform our understanding of society and the purposes of education. The outcomes of doing that heart-work and transformed understanding will prepare us to transform how we show up both with and for our students. It will prepare us to transform how we show up both with and for each other.

Such an appeal, laudable as it may be, would not make sense in anything other than a society that had deeply embraced a therapeutic revision of civic responsibility and public morality, while profoundly investing the epistemic authority of a certain therapeutic gaze. Heart-work, carried out in the privacy of an interior realm, too long avoided because of the discomfort it implies, is heart-work valorized according to a certain diagnostic logic. Such rhetoric engages in a unique collapsing of the public and private realms: we are to conduct a deeply intimate interrogation in response to and alongside what is an irreducibly public mandate, issued by one who knows, who sees into that bounded domain that constitutes our most intimate relation with ourselves. Indeed, the new racial sensibility precisely erases this boundary, making a public mandate of most private "heart-work."

The lens through which the therapeutic project of white reracialization is here considered is one that draws on Foucault's analysis of the ambivalent ways in which power operates through the production of subjects. One way to explain this is to take up the problem of the dispositif which we already encountered in the introductory chapter to this volume, and those modes of government through which its imperatives are enacted. As I have already argued, a dispositif is a mechanism through which a potentially disruptive force or intensity, something that resonates in the body or occurs in a shared resonance among several bodies, is simultaneously produced but also captured, excited but also controlled, its movement elicited but at the same time routed back to a safe, stable and reconciled location within an existing order. A dispositif is something that brings something to life, gives it power, capacity and force, but at the same time captures that force and contains it within a certain structure. Foucault defines the dispositif: "a thoroughly heterogeneous ensemble consisting of discourses, institutions, architectural forms, regulatory decisions, laws, administrative measures, scientific statements, philosophical, moral and philanthropic propositions," which combine in unique ways to regulate or capture social fields specifically by instating modes of subjectivity commensurate with the aims of the dispositif itself (Foucault, 1980, p. 194). Moreover, Foucault writes, the dispositif is a "formation which has as its major function at a given historical moment that of responding to an *urgent need*. The apparatus thus has a dominant strategic function." The panopticon, for Foucault, was a dispositif: it gave bodies utility and capacity in response to the need for public safety, but absorbed that capacity into the functioning of the factory, the prison, the school or the hospital. Sexuality was another of Foucault's dispositifs: it produced the sexual deviant, the homosexual, the hysterical female in a way that both inscribed these subjects with a certain force, but also drew that force back into a more controllable form. I will refer to this double movement of the dispositif as it pertains to the reracialization of whiteness: it displays a certain ambivalence or dynamism, which generates potentiality through the interiority it enacts, while at the same time subsuming that potential within an existing regime.

One of the most effective ways that the dispositif achieves this effect is through the operation of subjection—the process through which individuals are brought to look upon and accept themselves as certain kinds of subjects in certain kinds of ways, and to relate to themselves as people possessing a bounded interiority and a sense of self. This is a claim that specifically implicates the psychological sciences and the notion of interiority itself. Indeed, interiority as the effect of control is a notion that is central to Foucault's thought, one that, according to Foucault, extends beyond the human sciences to Christian theology, and to the notion of the soul. As Margaret McClaren puts it, "Soul, consciousness, psyche, subjectivity, and personality are each specific ways of conceptualizing human interiority" as forms of social control, an assertion that is summarized in one of Foucault's most notorious claims: "The soul is the effect and instrument of a political anatomy; the soul is the prison of the body" (McLaren, 2002, p. 81; Foucault, 1977, p. 31). For the purposes of the present discussion, it is enough to understand that this project of peering into the soul, of exploring ourselves as psychologized, racialized subjects of whiteness, is one that has the effect of simultaneously exciting and containing us, of mobilizing and immobilizing certain potentials within the white subjectivity that it seeks to remake.

Such ambivalence can also be read in another of Foucault's best-known treatments of this effect which will also serve to guide the present discussion and which we have already touched on in the previous chapter. In one of his most widely cited statements on the effects of subjection, Foucault plays on the multiple meanings of the word "subject" which, he contends, denotes a relation that binds together the personal with a relation of power: "There are two meanings of the word subject: subject to someone else by control and dependence, and [also] tied to his own identity by a conscience or self-knowledge. Both meanings suggest a form of power which subjugates and makes subject to" (Foucault, 1996, p. 331). In the same movement that one seeks to become a subject, that one goes in search of oneself through a process of self-reflection, one also becomes subject to the political rule of an ulterior political force, "tied" to a certain sought-after state of being, frozen in one's relation to oneself through one's subjugation to another. The Christian who probes his flesh for signs of his fallen nature, the pervert who studies his desires for clues to his psychic abnormality, the neoliberal subject who monitors his habits for vestiges of welfarist dependence or the psychiatric patient who examines his thoughts for telltale signs of madness, all share the experience of becoming subjects only through their immersion in a set of normalizing relations with the orders of psychiatry, sexology, entrepreneurship or Church doctrine. The inner relation they derive as subjects is at the same time subsumed within a relation to another, as being subject-to. Subjection as subject-to (I will employ this term with a hyphen to convey this designated use), may derive from the force of an authority or a superior power, though more likely it implies the imposition of a normalizing framework through which the self-relation of the subject is configured in a manner meant to impose some bio-normative expectation, and to contain any abnormal or aleatory deviation from its prescribed form. Under regimes of psychological government, for example, we are induced to study our inner life for subtle signs of deviation, and as such we become subject-to the normalizing effects of that regime we term psychology. Under these regimes, we accept that whatever we discover in ourselves, no matter how strange or unsettling, can ultimately be read back into the psychological template as "maladjusted," "neurotic," "OCD," "trauma," etcetera. Subjectivity arrives at, or is immediately brought back into, a relation to something that might be judged as normal or abnormal, as a problem that needs to be corrected, enhanced and understood, but also treated therapeutically.

It is through this relation of subordination, as subject-to that the subject becomes bound to a fictional self-identity. It is bound to itself through the imperative to develop the precise form of this inner relation, to discover, and through discovering to transform itself according to a specific protocol. One becomes a subject—acquires subjectivity, self-knowledge, insight into oneself, interiority—in the same movement that one enters into a set of relations of power and subordination. In fact, the operation of each depends on the function of the other: the more one accepts the terms of one's own inscrutability and the need to extract a unique and obtuse truth through the study of one's inner life, the more one enters into a relation of dependence on a whole network of experts and authorities poised to supervise this process. The more one invests the danger that one might develop abnormally, that one might betray the imperative of one's own psychic health, the more one finds oneself indebted to the assumptions and operational logics that demarcate abnormality and make possible the excavation of its secret. The more one is subject, the more one is also, and at the same time, subject-to. The invitation to "heart-work" is certainly an operation that brings together these two moments: the white subject is invited to develop a certain relation with herself, to overcome resistances, to confront secrets and to tolerate discomforts in order to get to the heart of an unhealthy soul, a soul that has gone wrong and grown aberrantly. In so doing she accepts herself as precisely such a subject of racial health, along with the normalizing assumptions and authorized knowledges that guide this important work. The more one undertakes such heart-work, the more one accepts the terms of one's self-interrogation, the more one finds oneself in the clutch of such systems of regulation whose overall investment is in sustaining this investigation as a certain ongoing, uninterrupted operational condition. Or, the more one seeks to uncover the secrets of one's white soul, as Foucault might have put it, the more this soul becomes the prison of the white body.

What must be remembered, and what one can derive from this Foucauldian perspective is that, organizationally, neither the white racial soul nor the racial dispositif has any interest in making obsolete the very problem around which it has received such veneration, even as the private sentiments and biographical experiences of the individuals staffing and populating this dispositif might reflect otherwise. It is certainly not in the interest of the diversity programs, the compilers of book lists, the publishers, the workshop leaders, the generators of pamphlets and brochures, blogs and websites, of the consultants and diversity coaches, the directors of human resources departments, of the Title IX officers and so on—it is not in the interest of the whole organizational edifice of the new racial sensibility that white racism should ever go away, even as racism itself might have brought great suffering to the lives of those individuals who work within these institutions. This edifice, as an organizational formation, inevitably frames racism not as a problem to be ended, overcome or transformed, but as one to be extended, reinvented in ever more infinitesimal forms, and ultimately managed—sustained indefinitely within the broader equilibrium of institutional life, and in such a way invested, animated, pursued and preserved. Racism today, in the hands of corporate consultants and diversity trainers, experts and ministers of white interiority has become a problem to be conserved precisely through the activity of an ongoing and unfolding interiority. To say as much is not to give way to cynicism so much as to acknowledge that the administrative form given to anti-racism behaves as any administrative form might—to administer, rather than to resolve, the problem over which it holds jurisdiction. Part of this managerial rationality requires that the subject engage in a constant and never-ending excavation of her most deeply held racial secrets, without actually changing itself in any way. Racism's multiplication and dissemination, its enduring refinement and differentiation into ever more insidious and discrete presences, has the indirect consequence of investing the white racist subject as the perfect managerial problem, the problem that never gets solved and the secret that never gets revealed, and of securing an indefinite expansion of the tactical fields of these managers themselves. This is Parkinson's law writ large.

By way of connecting these points, and to return to the problem of white reracialization, it is possible to claim that new processes of racialization, embedded as they are within a long tradition of therapeutic government, employ the problem of a secret inner life, of a great white inside, so as to secure this managerial equilibrium, and to return any incipient mutations of the white racial subject always back to the same unfolding problem, always back to the same iterations of white privilege, white ignorance or white supremacy and to the all-consuming core of whiteness itself. These terms function like enormous vacuum cleaners or as all-consuming black holes, sucking up and condensing all that might radiate out from the spontaneity of the social field back into the same secret white racism, and into the racial order itself. Interiority—or, that kind of interiority in that way—completes the circuit by which subjection maintains the subject as always subject-to. Thus, one of the key objectives of this study is to realize Foucault's assertion on the normalizing effects of psychiatric discipline on the level of a racial politics: the white soul becomes the prison of the white body.

3 Woke Reading and the Speechifying Effect

Central to Foucault's claim for the immobilizing effects of the *dispositif* is the property he affixes to discourse. Words, spoken and written, compose fields into which people are coerced once they begin to speak those words, reflecting a certain "incitement." When discursive fields frame the activity of self-inquiry, the effect of incitement is to align the inner lives of the subjects of discourse with the normative and normalizing effects of those fields, regulated as they are by experts, external authorities and prescriptive texts. In the first volume of the *History of Sexuality*, Foucault uses (at least in English translation) the awkward locution "speechifying" to describe the emergence of the subject into a discursive field, an event which involves "a whole machinery for speechifying, analyzing, and investigating" and through which "sex became something to say, and to say exhaustively in accordance with deployments that are varied, but all, in their own way, compelling" (Foucault, 1984, p. 32). As such, the dispositif brings about the fixing of the subject in processes of subjection, in part, by translating certain experiences into figures of language. Once people begin to speak of their encounters with themselves, particularly where those encounters imply some new contact with their own inner life, they are caught—bound to a definition of themselves from which they cannot escape. For this reason, it is important to explore the discursive field of the new racial sensibility, to uncover not just the governmental rationalities through which it operates but the unique relationship it establishes between experience and discourse, or between that which is sensed within, as a moment of inner reflection, and that which is regulated by language.

It cannot be denied that the new racial sensibility has a specific investment in the power of language to shape experience. Acronyms and neologisms drawn from social media replace everyday phrases, lending the new racial sensibility the aura of a certain vanguard. Only such new words, it is thought, have the capacity to name all those new objects and experiences that the new racial sensibility has brought to light. Yet at the same time that this language gives names to new social dimensions, it also tends to imbue these realms with a technical character that abolishes the ambiguity and flow that constitute their very social character itself. Read any apology issued by a public figure or institution in response to an embarrassing racial incident and one notices immediately how stale, formulaic and technical this speech can be, how labored the effort to make language perform the work of its unique moral alchemy, capturing and transforming raging discomfort into stable meanings. Through the lens of such language, the introspective mandate that defines so much of the new racial sensibility is inscribed as a technical operation. Indeterminacy and ambiguity are reduced in their nuance to the fixed points assigned by a prescriptive text. The inward gaze is always an uncertain one: one looks inside not knowing what one will find or what sort of change one's discoveries might ultimately bring. The willingness to peer inside oneself is also the willingness to be transformed by what one might discover, and to embark on a new and uncertain self-understanding. But put in technical language, this ambiguity is fixed—corralled and delimited. An encounter with some indeterminate element, one that instills an openness to who-knows-what, is, as Foucault says, "speechifed,"—remade through the grammar of language. What is said, felt and seen in the indeterminate space of self-reflection is contained within the safe parameters of a fixed code. As a problem of interiority, an unstable encounter with oneself is transformed by an outpouring of directives on the particularities of interiority itself. These include directives on correct anti-racist language use, on the need to continually renew language by dispensing with old or anachronistic terms, and on the safety afforded by the use of highly codified terms and phrases—all of which combine to reduce uncertain self-reflection to a technical exercise.

In the publishing world, a popular genre of nonfiction writing on race has drawn large numbers of readers to a set of titles variously engaged with the task of promulgating this new sensibility and its discursive effects. What one author termed the "literature of white liberalism" (Phruksachart, 2020) and others have termed "guilt lit," "white reading" or "woke lit," defines a hybrid discourse that bridges self-help and cultural commentary, counseling and popular psychology, activist how-to and the testimonial memoire (Roy, 2020). This genre includes titles such as Robin DiAngelo's *White Fragility: Why It's so Hard for White People to Talk About Racism*; Reni Eddo Lodge's *Why I'm No Longer Talking to White People About Racism*; Crystal Fleming's *How to Be Less Stupid About Race*; Ibram X. Kendi: *How to Be an Anti-Racist*; Ijeoma Oluo's *So You Want to Talk*

About Race; Layla Saad's *Me and White Supremacy: Combat Racism, Change the World, and Become a Good Ancestor* and many others. Though the publicly intended readership for this literature includes both white people and people of color, the problems to which woke lit is typically addressed and the transformations that it proposes seem best suited to the condition of whiteness itself. Crystal Fleming writes in her book *How to Be Less Stupid About Race*: "If you want to be an antiracist change agent, you're going to have to think long and hard about your own racial socialization… that's the kind of internal work that's required for addressing racism" (Fleming, 2018, p. 187). "Stupidity," in this sense, concerns a range of racial attitudes that might in theory be adopted by anyone, although it is difficult to avoid the implication that it is white people's racial stupidity that is at stake.

Woke lit gained a publishing foothold following a chain of high-profile racial incidents during the closing years of the Obama administration in the shadow of the emergent #BlackLivesMatter movement and ultimately with the election of Donald Trump in 2016. But it was with the uprisings in the spring of 2020 that a growing sense of the need to examine and transform deeply embedded habits associated with white racism brought this literature to the center of the national conversation (MacMullen, 2009; Ngo, 2017). Following a public outcry that flooded American cities with demonstrations and elicited public gestures of support from the highest offices of American business and administrative power, black activists intensified their demands that white society demonstrate meaningful solidarity with professed opposition to white supremacy. In the summer months of 2020, public acknowledgments of support for "black lives" sounded from the most unlikely sources: an enormous banner on the amazon.com website declaring "Black Lives matter: Amazon Stands With The Black Community" suggested the ease with which such gestures could be made, and the general suspicion that they lacked an integrity that could only be demonstrated through concrete action. As a consequence, within a certain public conversation, suspicious sensibilities were stoked, while solidarity, it was thought, should not be made so easy. Real solidarity had to involve the commitment of real resources and concrete political actions, but must also reflect the sort of integrity that can only come through a profound effort, a painful labor of self-examination. In fact, there is a sense conveyed throughout the new racial sensibility that the veracity of white self-reflection can only be certified through the evidence of a certain private white suffering. Whites have to really feel it, and it has to hurt, before their inner work can be verified, and the new woke reading would show the way by exposing readers to "uncomfortable truths." It is the scornful, paranoid other who would exercise this gatekeeping function, assuring that such suffering takes place. In the heady days of that summer, this new critical race literature would surge in popularity as recommended reading lists spawned like mushrooms across the internet (Kendi, 2019). Legacy newspapers, traditional magazines and online news sources, but also publishers, local book clubs, libraries and radio stations circulated lists of titles meant to induce racial self-reflection among whites. In June of 2020, it was possible for CNN to point out that "Amazon's Best Sellers List is Dominated Almost Entirely by Books on Race Right Now," reflecting the 15 race titles taking up the top 20 spots on that list (Andrews, 2020). Woke lit serves to abolish ambiguity, though the means by which it accomplishes this are quite specific. Woke lit cultivates a unique and precise suspicion through the presumption of a latent determination within the white psyche itself, or what Foucault called the "postulate of a general and diffuse causality": a suspicious belief that there is something down there causing a special kind of behavior, and that it is the task of the individual and the analyst to identify and redress this cause before the behavior can be accepted or excused (Foucault, 1984, p. 65). Faith in such a diffuse causality is deeply rooted in the contradictions of white racial liberalism as perceived by many people of color.

White involvement in anti-racist activism has always drawn scrutiny to the guile of the white activist (Applebaum, 2010). A storm of indignation from black bloggers on "performative allyship" in the wake of the George Floyd demonstrations highlighted the overwhelming insistence that white participation in anti-racist activism amounted to "virtue signaling," a thin surface papering over the deeper ego needs of activists themselves. This view was summarized in Robin DiAngelo's comment in an interview with Slate.com, "White Progressives are my specialty" (Jackson, 2019). Indeed, the affected shedding of "white tears" has generated its own literature, which comes with a strong admonition to deny empathy to what is undoubtedly a show, particularly when such tears are shed by women. Confronting white tears, one blogger writes: "I just take a big bucket outside and I use them to make Kool-Aid. ... You've never had a better glass of red Kool-Aid than one that's made with white tears" (Leah, 2018). Demands that whites prove their authenticity through some measure of emotional suffering have come from many sides: white integrity is to be shown through the setting aside of narcissistic preoccupations and turning to direct political action and solidarity work, usually in a supporting role within black social movements. Tre Johnson, in an article in the *Washington Post* writes: "When Black People are in Pain, White People Just Join Book Clubs" (Johnson, 2020). At other moments, however, it is these very public actions that are exposed for their conceit, as solicitations of black approval and appeals to an unearned moral insiderness in the eyes of other whites. Integrity, some allege, would be more convincingly demonstrated through the willingness to supplement public gestures with the more painful project of coming to "own one's privilege," through a confrontation with the hidden racism that constitutes one's indelible white secret. Such demands only intensified with the surge of interest in social justice literature in the months following the murder of George Floyd. For some, woke lit was precisely the means by which performative white solidarity could be made to show its mettle. Ibram Kendi encouraged precisely such reading as a means to, as he describes it, "dismantle this spurious legacy of our common upbringing" (Kendi, 2019). But for Kendi, authors of such readings should be wary of their own celebrity and suspicious even of those who read and publicly praise their books, for it is through such acceptance that white guile absorbs and neutralizes their most wrenching effects. Reading, many authors argued, should not spare the white reader some small measure of trauma. They should be books that are "difficult or unorthodox, that don't go down easily. Books that force us to confront our self-serving beliefs and make us aware that 'I'm not racist' is a slogan of denial." As in other cases, it is difficult to read this "us" as anything other than a polite way of saying "you" or "they," or as a euphemistic remonstration of whiteness itself.

Such "speechifying" of white racial discomfort extends well beyond the printed texts of woke lit. It occurs within a set of conversations, patterned on the therapeutic encounter, in which speech labors to both produce discomfort, while containing and subordinating any effects such discomfort might generate. In recent years, calls for conversation on topics of race have resonated across a range of American institutions, particularly those associated with education and government but also in media, commercial, corporate and business settings. The sense that these conversations are systematically avoided, that they are at once stressful for whites and tiresome for others, but that they are imperative if we are to get at deeper problems of racial inequality and yet ultimately impossible owing to the reluctance of whites to undertake them in earnest—these are all themes that permeate the new racial sensibility. Derald Wing Sue puts it this way in *Race Talk and the Conspiracy of Silence*: "Race talk threatens to unmask unpleasant and unflattering secrets about [white people's] roles in the perpetuation of oppression. Avoiding racial dialogues seems to have basic functions related to denial… Understanding the psychology of race talk from the perspective of white Americans and people of color has major implications for how educators and our society can use this knowledge to facilitate difficult dialogues on race" (Sue, 2015, p. 34). Silence, in this sense, is made into a form of speech, arrested and inscribed meaning as words withheld, and in this way, contained.

The ethics of discomfort that is so central to woke lit comprises an important commitment of the new racial sensibility: pain signals a reality that can only be derived through penetration into a deep interior realm, and this reality can never be entirely reduced to the discursive. Indeed, alongside white discomfort, black suffering is made to function as the measure of a certain truth, although in a very different manner from that of white discomfort. Where whiteness comprises the fog of self-ignorance, black suffering assumes the oracular function of a certain wisdom, a portal through which the painful interior realm of whiteness might be breached. In this sense, the truth-telling capacity of suffering derives a certain significance: the effect anthropologists have attributed to "social suffering" assumes a suffering that permanently eludes the interpretive schemes brought to bear on it and sustains as an ongoing limit to our ethical and empathic horizons (Kleinman et al., 1997). Black suffering, within the new racial sensibility, serves as precisely such a limit: it can be venerated as the object of loyalty and a thing of fealty, though it can never be known, cloaked as it is in a radical and irreducible difference. In this way, black suffering, as invoked by the new racial sensibility, is mobilized as the very condition of a certain unknowability, though one which points the way to a corresponding white introspection and self-knowledge. Knowing that one cannot know this suffering which nonetheless knows oneself all too well is a fact that maintains the mystery of white interiority as a permanent, ongoing and regenerating problem. Black suffering, as the inaccessible epistemic horizon of an Other one can never know but who knows one better than one can every know oneself, authorizes certain public acknowledgments that link an inaccessible white interiority with a declaration of public modesty. Statements such as "as a white male I can never know what it's like…" are gestures that invest black suffering as a kind of Delphic mirror through which one's own remote white secret is affirmed in a gesture that the philosopher Olúfẹ́mi Táíwò characterizes as a form of "epistemic deference" (Táíwò, 2020).

Read symptomatically, white pain confirms that the white subject has at last endeavored to take a look at itself through the eyes of an unreachable Other, if only fleetingly. Pain, or discomfort, administered scornfully and with resolve, certifies a reality that satisfies the suspicious regard. It is proof that the secret has been exhumed, at least in part, and that a truthful exposure has at least been attempted. But also, through this certification, the rhetoric of white discomfort confines the ambivalence of this exposure to specific coordinates. White discomfort is pain felt for a specific and precise interior state. The uncomfortable conversation with this interiority is meant to yield, through the suffering it induces, an epiphany or a sudden insight, though it is the kind of insight that comes about only through cathartic experience, as a form of relief one derives when one is at last released from the strictures of suffering and self-deception, and with a partial communion with the all-seeing Other. Cathartic truth releases tension, but it also completes a sort of cathartic labor, an undoing and redoing labor, the withstanding of a shock that brings relief and a newly sensitized consciousness. Thomas Scheff describes the cathartic effects that result from a session of psychotherapy: after an intense session, a client emerges from a state of "emotional inexpressiveness and rigidity" to one of "heightened sensory experience, and increased flexibility," having acquired a degree of self-distance from the intensity of the therapeutic experience itself (Scheff, 1979, p. 16). In this way, the solicitation of pain in listeners and readers is both the evidence and the instrument, both the cause and the effect of an insufferable exposure. Uncomfortable readings, like the uncomfortable discussions held in so many organizational settings, imply cathartic words, words that burn, and in their burning enact within the white reader a new inner relation. In this sense, the burn is ultimately a healing burn: administered to a reluctant patient by one possessing a certain medical authority, and with the intention of repairing an unhealthy mind and curing a pathological ignorance, applied as it is with a benevolence that befits a doctor.

4 The White Toothache

Anti-racist trainer Robin DiAngelo is perhaps the single-most celebrated public figure associated with the literary surge that followed the summer of racial reckoning. Her book, *White Fragility: Why It's So Hard for White People to Talk About Racism*, became a *New York Times* best seller and launched DiAngelo as the voice most widely associated with the new racial sensibility. To illustrate the meaning of the term white fragility, and the need to avoid the pitfalls of white defensiveness that such fragility implies, DiAngelo describes a contentious encounter with a woman of color with whom she collaborated on a research project. DiAngelo had offended this woman with a casual remark concerning an incident the day before in which a group of white office workers, when confronted with another colleague's black braided hair, had become anxious and unresponsive: "White people are scared of Deborah's hair," DiAngelo remarked. When word got back to her that her colleague had taken offense to this remark, DiAngelo reached out:

> I opened by asking Angela: "would you be willing to grant me the opportunity to repair the racism that I perpetrated toward you in that meeting?" When she agrees I continue. "I realize my comment about Deborah's hair was inappropriate." Angela nods and explains that she did not know me and did not want to be joking about black women's hair (a sensitive issue for many black women) with a white woman whom she did not have a trusting relationship with, much less in a professional work meeting.

DiAngelo apologizes, and the two move to conclude their discussion:

> I ask Angela if there is anything else that needs to be said or heard so that we may move forward. She replies that yes, there is. "The next time you do something like this, would you like feedback publicly or privately?" she asks. I answer that given my role as an educator, I would appreciate receiving the feedback publicly as it is important for white people to see that I am also engaged in a lifelong process of learning and growth. And could model for other white people how to receive feedback openly and without defensiveness. (140)

There is much in this exchange that a perceptive reader can learn about the new racial sensibility, not the least of which is the remarkable moral seriousness reflected in DiAngelo's circumspection and the resolute humility she displays in the face of what must have been an intense temptation to evade her colleague's concerns through deflection or explanation. DiAngelo is, without any doubt, modeling a new set of racial protocols, and in the course of doing so, making better social spaces for many people. Yet the limits of these protocols should also be noted, and some of their unanticipated functions pointed out. DiAngelo provides carefully fashioned interactive scripts which allow her to publicly model her engagement with the most private aspects of her racial being—her blindness to the needs of others, her insensitivity to the vulnerabilities of other racial groups, and in a more general sense what she would call her whiteness. However, the public self-censure she enacts is only achieved at the expense of a stifling suppression of the naturalness, and I would say the generativity, of shared interaction itself. In other words, DiAngelo is only able to open up this inner relation by sacrificing the indeterminate character of this interaction, consigning her self-interrogation to a certain ceremoniousness, a formal promulgation derived from the sort of scripted, managerial sociabilities which her workshops and her critical writings presume. Through such a lens, the new racial sensibility has come to imagine the ambivalent and multi-dimensional field of social and affective life only through the filter of a prescriptive therapeutic text, enacting a sociability heavily colonized by managerial imperatives, scripted self-renunciations and deferential gestures, which, I contend, ultimately yield only shallow exchanges easily corrected with starched language. In other words, DiAngelo's solution is one in which the interactive dynamic manifested in the shared co-presence of real bodies in real space, along with the very trauma and the sense of an inward glimpse induced by the racial encounter itself, is completely subsumed under a verbal protocol which she presents to her readers as complete and replicable, a perfect managerial solution to what might otherwise become a sticky and indeterminate social encounter. It is true that these scripts derive their ceremoniousness from what they imagine to be the deep work of white reconstruction, and from the work of a white interiority mentioned earlier. But notably, DiAngelo never tries to talk to this woman, to explain herself or to convey what she meant by her remark, or to engage her in any manner other that in complete deference to the epistemological and managerial authority implied by the inaccessibility of her suffering. While she is glad for the chance to inject her inner work into a public space (so that other white people can see that she is "also engaged in a lifelong process of learning and growth"), she doesn't actually include anyone else in that work as anything other than an authority presumed to already know her intentions, and thus as a director of appropriate technique. In this way this work remains constrained by a certain therapeutic imagination: a solitary engagement with her own innermost self through which the presence of the Other serves as a guide but also as a reflection, a screen onto which a certain authority is projected. In at least one sense, through this projection, the Other's presence is effaced. She accepts the woman's authority unquestioningly without actually engaging her presence—a positioning which, in a sense collapses the social space between them into a simple technical relation, a programmatic space, one in which the uncertainties of a complex encounter are, through their "speechification," relegated to a tidy outcome.

What the new racial sensibility often presents as a fully developed program of anti-racist civility derived from a reflexive reconstruction of the white racial subject is in fact a formal program that is incapable of addressing either the dynamic, slippery and indeterminate character of real interpersonal life or the nuanced, ambivalent and often traumatic ways in which subjects enter into painful practices of critical self-reflection. The Other, together with all the Other's suffering, becomes a managerial fiction, venerated as a perspective from which all truths are known. DiAngelo's insistence on a formalized protocol that folds together racial interaction and the work of white reconstruction into an integrated program suggests that the repudiation of her own conduct through public apology is a gesture that leaves only half the story told, that there continues an entirely different operation—a certain conservation, a reinvestment or a fondness for the very racial subject she so eloquently transcends. Indeed, DiAngelo's transcendence, and the cathartic self-distancing it implies, is so perfect, one wishes to see it enacted again and again. Amid her efforts to get it just right, to live out in real interactive space a fantasy concocted in words, what creeps in, it seems to me, is a sort of discursive eroticism, or a pleasure taken in the textual eloquence of the whole lived production. The operation of this discursive erotics, a cathecting of the secret-to-be-disclosed in which the actual presence of the Other is reduced to a fiction, is apparent across the whole surface of the new racial sensibility. The pathological condition of white racism becomes an object of erotic investment, a love for the sick self-to-be-cured. Such an eroticism is captured by Freud in his description of the plight of a sick person who, preoccupied with their sickness, becomes narcissistic, withdrawing libidinal investment from their surrounding world while focusing inwardly on the source of their pain. What he terms the "familiar egoism of the sick person" is reflected in a line of comic verse in which a lover who, afflicted with a toothache, turns his attention from his loved object to the source of his discomfort: "concentrated is his soul on his molar's aching hole" (Freud, 1925, p. 82). Whiteness as tooth-ache implies a white subject who has fallen in love with her own sickness—the sickness of a whiteness from which she yearns to escape, yet which sustains as a perverse object of captivating investment.

On this point the elements of my critique of the new racial sensibility begin to converge: there is a sense in which the problems posed by this form of therapeutic reason, of an interiority induced and captured, of a traumatic convulsion harnessed and drawn into the realm of language, are not really meant to be resolved, but instead are made to operate in a way that preserves a certain equilibrium. The suspicious gaze and the obscure racial interior, as they fold together in the new racial sensibility, attain a certain equipoise, a discursive erotics, in which gestures of exposure and experiences of discomfort assume a performative significance that bypasses, even inhibits any meaningful shift in the relative positions of a racial subjectivity—and by implication of the racial order itself. Through its formalization as a discursive enactment of a white interiority shaped around practices of concealment and exposure, the uncomfortable conversation has attained a heaviness and weight that sustains the bad racist subject it needs, while suppressing all the plasticity, the mobility and the possible lines of escape that might develop from the dynamic field of racial sociability itself. To say this is not to add to the now familiar refrain that white people haven't done enough to divest themselves of their racism, that, even in their most public gestures of transcendence there operates a sinister subterfuge through which whiteness preserves itself, that DiAngelo is in fact indulging a hidden white narcissism at the expense of some other more authentic mode of anti-racist solidarity, etcetera. The claim is not that these confessional gestures are "merely performative" or that some even more painful, even more intense and even more authentic exposure must be extracted if white people are to finally enact a true disclosure of their white secrets. I do not wish to redouble the inflationary rhetoric that undergirds the program of the new racial sensibility, to make another, more clever call out of the more clever ruse of a white racial renunciation that deviously withholds some last secret from its interrogators. I will leave that task to the debunking tradition of paranoid critique that I have already stated my intention to avoid. Instead, I wish precisely to think outside of the logic of the therapeutic interiority upon which such charges depend, to mark the limitations of this logic and even, indirectly, to consider some alternatives. It's not that white people haven't done enough to betray the secrets of their racism, or haven't done it with enough sincerity or with enough discomfort. The claim is that perhaps they (or at least some small number of them) have in fact done too much, with a sincerity that solicits trauma in a way that leads them to invest that trauma itself. It's not that they haven't practiced enough sincerity or delved deeply enough into their shadowy interiors, but that they have done so with a faith and a devotion, and through a technical apparatus, that itself serves the ends of a certain distancing, a formalizing perfection that, by maintaining the Other and the Other's suffering in the role of a certain therapeutic omniscience, sustains all those key elements that define the classic features of white racism itself—the confining of the Other to the role of a radical racial alterity contrived in such a way as to consolidate the existential needs of an unstable white subject, even where such consolidation implies the bringing of discomfort. Indeed, it is perhaps this white racial optic that sustains the link between the old white racialization and the new: the Other remains Other, framed by an alterity that puts it to work, again, as the mirror of a white racial subject. White anti-racists have taken up the anti-racist program too much on its own terms, pursued it too faithfully, too schematically, embraced it as a totalizing ideology and as a managerial technique, and in so doing have produced and fallen in love with the very subject that is the target of that project itself, like a tongue endlessly washing over an aching tooth. The moral certainty under which the new racial sensibility labors, and the rigidity of the epistemic lens through which it extracts its truths all mobilize against another level of experience, one rooted not in the discursive form but in the affective currents and the modes of intersubjective life that course through the process of racialization itself. In the new racial sensibility, a therapeutic reason subsumes the dynamic potentials that might otherwise have emerged from some other inner encounter, one undertaken in relation to a more open field of affect, oriented to the very potentiality inscribed in racial sociability itself as a mode of shared public existence. And perhaps, through some obscure consensus, that is its purpose. To ensure that the erotic labor of white interiority will continue indefinitely, that it will snuff out the possibilities of a generative social field as it is played out again and again, with the assurance that there will always remain some vestige of white racism to expose, to painfully confront, that the authoritative, all-seeing racial Other will preside over this process and that this act of exposure will be performed, *ad infinitum* and *ad nauseam*. All of this ensures that the racial order and all of its comfortable discomforts will ultimately remain in a relation of perpetual balance—the perfect managerial object.

A reader could be forgiven at this point for concluding that what lies ahead is a very Foucauldian read. Such a read might go something like this: these new racializations of whiteness that go by the name of the new racial sensibility have gone to bed with all those technologies of interiority that invest our modern psychological society, and consequently have the effect of disciplining our racial selves in ways we don't acknowledge. They do this by seducing us into the task of making white racism speak, of capturing it in words which have the undeclared effect of producing precisely the racial subject they purport only to uncover. As a consequence, they yield what promises to be a more concerted engagement with white racism. But, ah ha! viewed through my clever Foucauldian lens, this engagement turns out to be a more thorough incorporation of racial structures themselves. Such a reading would mean recasting as a problem of race those things that Foucault so famously said about sexuality and the repressive hypothesis: "Did the critical discourse that addresses itself to repression come to act as a roadblock to a power mechanism that had operated unchallenged up to that point, or is it not in fact part of the same historical network as the thing it denounces" (Foucault, 1984, p. 10). My response would be that yes, the reracialization of whiteness, while transmitting many varied effects, many of which are quite valuable for the overcoming of racial inequalities in public life, through its veneration of the Other, also serves to reproduce key features of the problem of white racism itself, that it participates in the "same historical network as the thing it denounces." The white racial hypothesis that will be examined in this book is one that succeeds in always ensuring that no real alternative to this white racist subject will be tolerated, as all possible alternatives have already been anticipated, captured, called out and folded back into the all-encompassing task of stripping yet another mask from the masquerade that is white racial conceit. Such would be the Foucauldian book that could lie ahead, and, yes, in what follows, this story is certainly apparent, and provides much of the general framework for what lies ahead. However, within this framework, and in many ways against the grain of this Foucauldian story, there is a turn in store that will place the discussion on a very different footing.

First, on the question of power as a discursive effect, an important departure in the pages that follow will concern my willingness to turn from the predominantly discursive framework that Foucault employs to a wider consideration of affect and emotion, and specifically to the affective states that apply to a material sense of racial embodiment. Whiteness and its reracialization, interiority and the effects of exposure that operate at the heart of the new racial sensibility are not, I will argue, simply the product of a certain incitement to discourse, the speechifying effect of an apparatus, a dispositif that deploys from above, as it sometimes seems in Foucault's work. The traumatic self-encounter that characterizes a certain moment of white self-reflection and that the motif of interiority helps to suppress are, I will argue, already deeply inscribed in the somatic, material experiences of white racial existence. Whiteness and its contemporary reracialization are only the particular historical refinements of this racial being. Race, after all, while it owes a lot to words, is also about flesh—skin, hair and eyes, but also blood, genes and what we think of as biology. The very modes of embodiment implied by race, the ways in which race develops a unique sense of the materiality of subjective life through processes of racialized sociability, I will argue, already invoke their own play of concealment and exposure, and their own appeal to an underlying interiority upon which the new racial sensibility only imposes its own particular stamp. In other words, race already has its own non-discursive, or perhaps co-discursive sense of embodiment, and in describing this embodiment I am suggesting, *contra* Foucault the discursive constructionist, that white interiority and its hidden secrets might be considered through a somatic lens that takes into account the affective and material dimensions of the racializing process in a more general sense.

More precisely, in what is to follow, the moments of subject and subject-to that compose the process of white reracialization, the effects of shock and capture and the function of the dispositif that inscribes movement in order to recuperate that movement back into itself—this dynamic double movement will be transcribed from a Foucauldian problematic of desire and its capture in speech into one defined by a critical conversation on the affect of shame (Leys, 2007; Sedgwick & Frank, 1995). Shame, I will argue, has a lot to tell us about race, but also it has a lot to say about the tension between inside and outside, secrecy and exposure, between that which remains hidden and that which is open to public view, and about the compulsion to render this inside transparent through therapeutic confession and disclosure. Indeed, the shameful encounter implied by white reracialization will be considered as a diffuse trauma, a fragility and an occasion for white tears, which opens up new, unstable and often traumatic encounters, subjectivities that remain ultimately outside and beyond the recuperative scope of racialization processes and their regulative texts. And it is because of the traumatic character brought on by this shame, and because of the instability it enacts, that the shame of white reracialization is quickly "interiorized," ensnared within another affective regime, one characterized not by a generative shame but by a normalizing sense of guilt, and the discursive, speechified forms through which guilt operates. Just as one's racial self, exposed in shame, both opens up and constrains a subject, so shame, it will be argued, has a way of flipping, or transmuting from a painful encounter with itself into a resolute commitment to repair one's inner being—a commitment that derives from a dutiful sense of guilty responsibility to the Other. Guilt for one's pathological inner life, an alluring and repugnant interiority, allows the subject to avoid shame's trauma, and with it all the difficult confrontations trauma invokes. So the double movement that incorporates an undermining of the white racial subject with the consolidation of a racial order will be played out in the transmutation of a shame that is reexperienced as guilt (Lewis, 1971b; Scheff, 1994). With these concerns in mind, it is to this indeterminate realm of racial shame that we now turn.

References

Ahmed, S. (2012). *On Being Included: Racism and Diversity in Institutional Life.* Duke University Press.

Ahmed, S. (2007). A Phenomenology of Whiteness. *Feminist Theory, 8*(2), 149–168.

Alcoff, L. M. (1999). Toward a Phenomenology of Racial Embodiment. *Radical Philosophy, 95*, 15–26.

Alcoff, L. M. (2015). *The Future of Whiteness.* Polity Press.

Allport, G. (1979). *Nature of Prejudice*, 25th anniversary edition. Perseus.

Anand, R., & Winters, M.-F. (2008). A Retrospective View of Corporate Diversity Training From 1964 to the Present. *Academy of Management Learning & Education, 7*(3), 356–372.

Andrews, S. (2020, June 3). Amazon's Best Sellers List is Dominated Almost Entirely by Books on Race Right Now. *CNN.* Retrieved June 12 2023, from https://www.cnn.com/2020/06/03/us/amazon-best-sellers-books-race-trnd/index.html

Appiah, A. (1996). Race, Culture, Identity: Misunderstood Connections. In A. Appiah & A. Gutman (Eds.), *Color Conscious.* Princeton University Press.

Applebaum, B. (2010). *Being White, Being Good: White Complicity, White Moral Responsibility, and Social Justice Pedagogy*. Lexington.

Aware L. A. (2021). Unmasking Whiteness Institute. Retrieved June 12 2023, from https://www.awarela.org/unmasking-whiteness-institute

Balibar, E. (2011). Is There a 'Neo-Racism'? In E. Balibar & I. Wallerstein (Eds.), *Race, Class, Nation: Ambiguous Identities*. Verso.

Bernasconi, R., & Lott, T. (2000). *The Idea of Race*. Hackett.

Binkley, S. (2015). *Happiness as Enterprise: an Essay on Neoliberal Life*. SUNY Press.

Binkley, S. (2016). Anti-racism Beyond Empathy: Transformations in the Knowing and Governing of Racial Difference. *Subjectivity, 9*, 181–204.

Binkley, S. (2019a). Black Rage and White Listening: On the Psychologization of Racial Emotionality. In E. Severson, D. Goodman, & H. Macdonald (Eds.), *Race, Rage and Resistance*. Routledge.

Binkley, S. (2019b). Unlearning Privilege: The Therapeutic Ethos and the Battle Within the White Self. In D. Nehring, O. Jacob Madsen, E. Cabanas, C. Mills & D. Kerrigan (Eds.), *Handbook of Global Therapeutic Cultures*. Routledge.

Burchell, G. (1996). Liberal Government and Techniques of the Self. In A. Barry, T. Osborne, & N. Rose (Eds.), *Foucault and Political Reason*. UCL Press.

Chang, A., Martin, R., & Marrapodi, E. (2020). Summer of Racial Reckoning. Podcast. Retrieved June 12 2023, from https://www.npr.org/2020/08/16/902179773/summer-of-racial-reckoning-the-match-lit

Cherry, F. (2000). The Nature of 'The Nature of Prejudice'. *Journal of the History of Behavioral Sciences, 36*(4), 489–498.

Cross, W. E. (1971). The Negro-to-Black Conversion Experience. *Black World, 20*(9), 13–27.

Dean, M. (1999). *Governmentality: Power and Rule in Modern Society*. Sage.

DiAngelo, R. (2018). *White Fragility: Why It's So Hard For White People To Talk About Racism*. Beacon Press.

Dyer, R. (1988). White. *Screen, 29*(7), 44–64.

Fleming, C. (2018). *How to Be Less Stupid About Race: On Racism, White Supremacy, and the Racial Divide*. Beacon Press.

Foucault, M. (1984). *The History of Sexuality, Volume 1, An Introduction* (R. Hurley, Trans.). Vintage Books.

Foucault, M. (1991). Governmentality (R. Braidotti, Trans., and C. Gordon, Revised). In G. Burchell, C. Gordon, & P. Miller (Eds.), *The Foucault Effect: Studies in Governmentality* (pp. 87–104). University of Chicago Press.

Foucault, M. (1977). *Discipline and Punish: The Birth of the Prison*. Pantheon Books.

Foucault, M. (1980). The Confession of the Flesh. In C. Gordon, T. C. Gordon, L. Marshall, J. Hepham, & K. Soper (Eds.), *Power/Knowledge: Selected Interviews and other Writings 1972–1977*. Pantheon.

Foucault, M. (1996). The Subject and Power. In J. D. Faubion (Ed.), *Michel Foucault: Power* (R. Hurley & Others, Trans.). The New Press.

Fredrickson, G. M. (2002). *Racism: A Short History*. Princeton University Press.

Freud, S. (1925). On Narcissism: An Introduction. In J. Strachey et al. (Ed. and Trans.), *The Standard Edition of the Psychological Works of Sigmund Freud* (pp. 79–104, vol. 14). Hogarth.

Gilman, S., & Thomas, J. (2016). *Are Racists Crazy? How Prejudice, Racism and Antisemitism Became Markers of Insanity.* New York University Press.

Global Industry Analysts. (2021, November 3). With Global Spending Projected to Reach $15.4 Billion by 2026, Diversity, Equity & Inclusion Takes the Lead Role in the Creation of Stronger Businesses. *Cision PR Wire.* Retrieved June 12 2023, from https://www.prnewswire.com/news-releases/with-global-spending-projected-to-reach-15-4-billion-by-2026%2D%2Ddiversity-equity%2D%2Dinclusion-takes-the-lead-role-in-the-creation-of-stronger-businesses-301413808.html

Goldberg, D. T. (1993). *Racist Culture: Philosophy and the Politics of Meaning.* Blackwell.

Helms, J. (1984). Toward a Theoretical Explanation of the Effects of Race on Counseling: A Black and White Model. *The Counseling Psychologist, 72*(4), 153–165.

Helms, J. (1991). *A Training Manual to Accompany Black and White Racial Identity.* Content Communications.

Ignatiev, N. (1995). *How the Irish Became White.* Routledge.

Illouz, E. (2008). *Saving the Modern Soul: Therapy, Emotions, and the Culture of Self-Help.* University of California Press.

Irving, D. (2014). *Waking Up White, and Finding Myself in the Story of Race.* Elephant Room Press.

Jackson, L. M. (2019, September 4). What's Missing From White Fragility. *Slate Magazine.* Retrieved June 12 2023, from https://slate.com/human-interest/2019/09/white-fragility-robin-diangelo-workshop.html

Johnson, T. (2020, June 11). When Black People are in Pain, White People Just Join Book Clubs. *Washington Post.* Retrieved June 12 2023, from https://www.washingtonpost.com/outlook/white-antiracist-allyship-book-clubs/2020/06/11/9edcc766-abf5-11ea-94d2-d7bc43b26bf9_story.html

Katz, J. H. (1978). *White Awareness: Handbook for Anti-Racist Training.* University of Oklahoma Press.

Kendi, I. X. (2019, May 29). Ibram X. Kendi's Antiracist Reading List. *New York Times.* Retrieved June 12 2023, from https://www.nytimes.com/2019/05/29/books/review/antiracist-reading-list-ibram-x-kendi.html

Kirwan Institute for the Study of Race and Ethnicity. (2012). Understanding Implicit Bias, May 29. Retrieved June 12 2023, from https://kirwaninstitute.osu.edu/article/understanding-implicit-bias

Kleinman, A., Das, V., & Lock, M. M. (1997). *Social Suffering.* University of California Press.

Kovel, J. (1984). *White Racism: A Psychohistory.* Columbia University Press.

Lasch-Quinn, E. (2002). *Race Experts: How Racial Etiquette, Sensitivity Training, and New Age Therapy Hijacked the Civil Rights Revolution*. Rowman & Littlefield.

Leah, D. (2018). When The 'White Tears' Just Keep Coming. *Code Switch: Race in Your Face*. Retrieved June 12 2023, from https://www.npr.org/sections/codeswitch/2018/11/28/649537891/when-the-white-tears-just-keep-coming

Lewis, Helen B. (1971b). *Shame and Guilt in Neurosis*. International Universities Press.

Leys, R. (2007). *From Guilt to Shame: Auschwitz and After*. Princeton University Press.

MacMullen, T. (2009). *Habits of Whiteness: A Pragmatist Reconstruction*. Indiana University Press.

Mallon, R. (2004). Passing, Traveling and Reality: Social Constructionism and the Metaphysics of Race. *Nous, 38*(4), 644–673.

McLaren, M. A. (2002). *Feminism, Foucault, and Embodied Subjectivity*. SUNY Press.

McWhorter, J. (2017, April 14). Anti-racism: Our Flawed New Religion. *Daily Beast*. Retrieved June 12 2023, from https://www.thedailybeast.com/antiracism-our-flawed-new-religion

McWhorter, J. (2021, July 31). The Great Awokening. *The Weeds*, podcast. Retrieved June 12 2023, from https://podcasts.apple.com/us/podcast/the-great-awokening/id1042433083?i=1000486672252

McWhorter, L. (2005). Where do White People Come From? A Foucaultian critique of Whiteness Studies. *Philosophy and Social Criticism, 31*(5–6), 533–336.

McWhorter, L. (2009). *Racism and Sexual Oppression in Anglo-America: A Genealogy*. Indiana University Press.

Metzl, J. (2019). *Dying of Whiteness: How the Politics of Racial Resentment is Killing America's Heartland*. Basic Books.

Ngo, H. (2017). *The Habits of Racism: A Phenomenology of Racism and Racialized Embodiment*. Lexington.

Nolan, J. (1998). *The Therapeutic State: Justifying Government at Century's End*. New York University Press.

Oluo, I. (2019). *So You Want To Talk About Race?* Seal Press.

Omi, M., & Winant, H. (1994). *Racial Formation in the United States: From the 1960s to the 1990s* (2nd ed.). Routledge.

Phruksachart, M. (2020, August 21). The Literature of White Liberalism. *Boston Review*. Retrieved June 12 2023, from https://bostonreview.net/race/melissa-phruksachart-literature-white-liberalism

Roediger, D. (1991). *The Wages of Whiteness: Race and the Making of the American Working Class*. Verso.

Rose, N. (1990). *Governing the Soul: The Shaping of the Private Self*. Routledge.

Rose, N. (1999). *Powers of Freedom: Reframing Political Thought*. Cambridge University Press.

Roy, S. (2020, September 9). Guilt Lit. *Los Angeles Review of Books*. Retrieved June 12 2023, from https://lareviewofbooks.org/short-takes/guilt-lit/

Scheff, T. (1979). *Catharsis in Healing, Ritual and Drama*. Iuniverse.

Scheff, T. (1994). *Bloody Revenge: Emotions, Nationalism and War*. iUniverse.

Schwartzman, P. (2016). Why Some Whites are Waking up to Racism. *Washington Post*. Retrieved June 12 2023, from https://www.washingtonpost.com/local/social-issues/why-some-whites-are-waking-up-to-racism/2016/08/03/5f2c2386-5051-11e6-aa14-e0c1087f7583_story.html

Sedgwick, E. K., & Frank, A. (1995). *Shame and its Sisters: A Silvan Tomkins Reader*. Duke University Press.

Sennett, R. (1976). *The Fall of Public Man*. Norton & Company.

Sue, D. W. (2015). *Race Talk and the Conspiracy of Silence: Understanding and Facilitating Difficult Dialogues on Race*. Wiley.

Sullivan, S. (2006). *Revealing Whiteness: The Unconscious Habits of Racial Privilege*. Indiana University Press.

Sullivan, S. (2015). *Good White People: The Problem with Middle-class White Anti-Racism*. SUNY Press.

Táíwò, O. (2020, December). Being-In-The-Room Privilege: Elite Capture and Epistemic Deference. *The Philosopher*. Retrieved June 12 2023, from https://www.thephilosopher1923.org/post/being-in-the-room-privilege-elite-capture-and-epistemic-deference

Thomas, D. A., & Ely, R. J. (1996). Making Differences Matter: A New Paradigm for Managing Diversity. *Harvard Business Review*. Retrieved June 12 2023, from https://hbr.org/1996/09/making-differences-matter-a-new-paradigm-for-managing-diversity

Wise, T. (2010). *Colorblind: The Rise of Post-Racial Politics and the Retreat from Racial Equity*. City Lights Books.

Wise, T. (2011). *White Like Me: Reflections on Race from a Privileged Son*. Soft Skull Press.

Yancy, G. (2004). A Foucauldian (Genealogical) Reading of Whiteness: The Production of the Black Body/Self and the Racial Deformation of Pecola Breedlove in Toni Morrison's The Bluest Eye. In G. Yancy (Ed.), *What White Looks Like: African-American Philosophers on the Whiteness Question*. Routledge.

Yglesias, M. (2019, April 1). The Great Awokening: A Hidden Shift is Revolutionizing American Racial Politics—and Could Transform the Future of the Democratic Party. The Highlight by *Vox*. Retrieved June 12 2023, from https://www.vox.com/2019/3/22/18259865/great-awokening-white-liberals-race-polling-trump-2020

Zack, N. (2002). *Philosophy of Science and Race*. Routledge.

CHAPTER 3

White Shame and Racial Abandonment

Abstract Having established a certain pattern of white racial subjection composed of the elements of shame and guilt, this chapter considers the first of these moments, the moment of white shame, which is central to the new racial sensibility and to the effect of white subjection it imposes. Calling on the work of shame theorists (Tomkins, Scheff and others), it is argued that white racial shame as administered in the new racial sensibility imposes a small moment of trauma in which the white subject experiences himself and the broader social field in the light of a certain novelty. This novelty, or social productivity, is one that contains a specific potential for an anti-racist project which seeks to interrogate and transform white subjectivity itself.

Keywords Shame • Silvan Tomkins • Thomas Scheff • Blushing • Whiteness • Abandonment

In 2018, a letter was published in the *New York Times* under the title "How Can I Cure My White Guilt?". The author, identified only as "Whitey," shares profound feelings of regret deriving from his or her reflection on their personal condition of whiteness. After having spent years in racially diverse educational settings, Whitey joined the largely white student body at an elite private college where Whitey's whiteness became an unbearably toxic presence, something he or she struggled to

S. Binkley, *Against White Interiority*,
https://doi.org/10.1007/978-3-031-31828-3_3

confront every day. Notwithstanding a solid record of anti-racist *bona fides*, Whitey describes a deep sense of shame that attaches to the problem of white being, and to the feelings of harm this state seems to broadcast to all those around: "I'm riddled with shame. White shame… I feel like my literal existence hurts people, like I'm always taking up space that should belong to someone else."

> I don't talk about my feelings because it's hard to justify doing so while people of color are dying due to systemic racism and making this conversation about me would be again centering whiteness. Yet bottling it up makes me feel an existential anger that I have a hard time channeling since I don't know my place. Instead of harnessing my privilege for greater good, I'm curled up in a ball of shame. How can I be more than my heritage? (Strayed & Almond, 2018)

What is striking in this passage is that Whitey has done nothing wrong. There is no action for which Whitey could issue an apology or make amends. It is Whitey's being that is the problem, a being Whitey is painfully unable to transcend. Indeed, there is something of a spiral effect in Whitey's shame: he or she feels shame for the very physicality of white being, but also shame from the very conundrum attending to the presence of shame feelings themselves, as if white shame were itself a thing of unique and repugnant materiality, taking up valuable space: "[My shame] isn't helpful to me or to anyone, especially people of color. I feel like there is no 'me' outside of my white/upper middle class/cisgender identity." Whitey's spiral, a shame about shame, is a curious one, reflecting an almost panicked need to escape a body to which one is unbearably bound. Indeed, as I shall argue here, Whitey's panic expresses a shame that is more general to racial life itself, although here filtered through the lens of a certain white panic spurred by a fearful and horrible glimpse into one's own inner being.

Race, according to a certain classical conception that is still very much with us today, is a human attribute that never entirely disentangles itself from the threat of shame. This is not to say that shame is race's exclusive domain: women, queers, the differently abled and many others consigned to the margins of social membership are done so not only for their actions but in the name of the very shamefulness of their being—a point that is reflected in various literatures on shame, affect and embodiment which compose this discussion (Schefer & Munt, 2019; Dolezol, 2016).

Nonetheless, some specification of shame's function in this particular case is possible: through this classical conception, the very idea of race conveys a sense of necessity, a rootedness in the materiality of our embodiment that runs contrary to modern beliefs in the sovereignty of human comportment. According to this view, to undertake some form of public conduct, that is, to do something civically, is to do it freely, through the sovereignty of one's choice and in full mastery of one's impulses and bodily sensations. On the other hand, to do something racially is to do in accordance with forces one cannot control and of which one is not fully aware, forces rooted in the material essence of one's being. As Charles Mills has argued, race aligns with those very states of nature which modern civil societies conspire to exclude through the formation of social contracts. Contracts are understandings and chosen agreements forged on the basis of elected behaviors that are presumed to be free, fair and reasonable (Mills, 1999). Those marked by race are excluded from civic life for the biological necessity to which they are bound, which makes such freedom impossible. As such, race troubles the subject who would enter into this contract. Race insists on the unfreedoms that underpin public conducts, deriving as they do not from our reflective choices but from states of bodily being and hereditary nature. To have the freedom of one's choices revealed as scripted by a great unfreedom, a materiality of which one is unaware is a shock and a degradation, and it is through this shock that race troubles and disrupts the raced subject even as we contest race's most basic assumptions (Bernasconi, 2001; Bernasconi & Lott, 2000). For people of color such shame results principally from the perpetual reactivation of psychic wounds that are the consequence of racist violence, however subtle or symbolic, particularly as this shame surfaces in response to the conduct of white people whose obstinate attitudes draw a sense of hopelessness and exhaustion (Bouson, 2000). But also, as Whitey's letter demonstrates, there is white racial shame, though this trouble is often less localized, an indistinct affect that is not so easily bound by the topography of the wound or attributable to the actions of a concrete Other. White racial shame is alternately chronic and acute, at times a diffuse and phantom-like swelling and dissipating that disquiets the white subject from no place in particular, while at other times it is a sudden eruption, a seizure that plunges the panicked subject into a morass of irreconcilable fears, desires and rationalizations. It is the diffuse character of white shame that gives it its force as a deracializing agent, a shock that threatens, or promises to remake whiteness itself, and with it the racial order in its entirety.

The reracialization of whiteness described in the previous chapter, I have argued, operates through such feelings of shame and animates those explosions of white fragility that Robin DiAngelo has so well documented and which so many white people undergo in the moment that they discover themselves raced. Such responses are described: "anger, fear, and guilt, and behaviors such as argumentation, silence, and leaving the stress-inducing situation. These behaviors, in turn, function to reinstate white racial equilibrium" (DiAngelo, 2018, p. 57). Martin-Alcoff has attributed this panic to what she terms the "turmoil of white subjectivity," a condition that follows from a changing racial order in which whites "find themselves the object of a new gaze that foregrounds their whiteness in ways that are not always flattering," (Martin-Alcoff, 2015, p. 140; Yancy, 2012). Moreover, within the literatures that compose the new racial sensibility, this panic is widely acknowledged not just as an emotional but as a bodily effect: Reni Eddo-Lodge, a UK-based commentator on race issues whose 2017 book *Why I'm No Longer Talking to White People About Race* grew from a 2014 blog post to become a major best seller, describes the physiological changes that come over white people as they struggle in conversations about race:

> Their eyes glaze over in boredom or widen in indignation. Their mouths start twitching as they get defensive. Their throats open up as they try to interrupt, itching to talk over you but not really listen, because they need to let you know that you've got it wrong. (Eddo-Lodge, 2017, p. ix)

In these moments, racial shame, the moment of shock described in the introduction of this volume, suffuses white bodily life, though it is also an affect quickly attended to, as I have already described, through a series of reactions meant to enact a certain capture or concealment, to arrest its movement or to hide shame behind a veil of words. W.E.B. DuBois, in the opening paragraphs of *Souls of Black Folks*, describes the sense of unease with which well-meaning white colleagues approach him "in a half-hesitant sort of way." There is a question for which they struggle to find the right words, a question that is typically avoided, "unasked by some through feelings of delicacy; by others through the difficulty of rightly framing it. All, nevertheless, flutter round it." In this fluttering, Dubois tells us, the question itself, "How does it feel to be a problem" gets asked only indirectly in an array of comments ("I know an excellent colored man in my town") that today might be registered as inappropriate (DuBois, 1994). Alison Bailey interprets this fluttering as an effort at concealment for that which the subject feels guilt. It is a uniquely motivated flight from responsibility, and an avoidance that is meant to allow only a surface-level engagement with the ultimate responsibility the white subject shoulders for their complicity with the existing racial order (Bailey, 2015, 2021). Bailey usefully identifies many of the behavioral features of this fluttering guilt: "We flutter when we resist lighting upon or dwelling in spaces where we feel unsafe and vulnerable. We flutter when we look for detours, distract ourselves, and pull into our bodies. We flutter when we blame others, become defensive, or treat people of color as our confessors" (Bailey, 2021, p. 40). Fluttering, in this sense, shrouds unsightly white failings behind a screen of language. It is the concealment of an internal moral flaw, a panicked response to a perceived exposure that is meant to avoid responsibility for a history of action one does not wish the Other to see and perhaps one does not wish to see oneself.

Such flutter induces a fitful pattern of conversational evasion and fluster identified by Alice McIntyre as "white talk," through which the white subject seeks vindication, aiming to restore a white comfort that is preserved only at the cost of cognitive stability. Sometimes white talk is defensive: "derailing the conversation, evading questions, dismissing counterarguments, withdrawing from the discussion, remaining silent, interrupting speakers and topics, and colluding with each other in creating a 'culture of niceness' that make[s] it very difficult to 'read the white world'" (McIntyre, 1997, p. 46). Though at other times it dissolves into a chattery rationalization, a panicked need to clarify in words that which has been so unsettlingly activated in feelings. Often white talk becomes confessional and overly personal, attaining a level of intimacy not warranted by the situation, seeking to control the disclosure of one's white secrets through the divulgence of some hastily fashioned truth designed to take the place of some far more unsettling inner discovery. This flutter and the talk it conveys gives us a sense of the "speechifying" effect of discourse that Foucault pointed to and which we observed in the previous chapter. However, while these authors interpret flutter and white talk as an effort to conceal feelings of guilt deriving from white complicity with a skewed racial order, I read these as expressions differently. White flutter is not, or not just, an expression of guilt, but also of shame—affects attaching not to the deeds but to the very materiality of white racial being itself. Whitey's flutter, if that's what it is, serves not to conceal the deviousness of what Whitey has done, for Whitey hasn't done anything. It serves to halt a spiraling dread resulting from a shameful encounter with what one is.

In the introduction to this book I described the two moments of white subjection imposed through the function of the new racial sensibility. Shock and capture, or shock that succumbs to capture (also read through a Foucauldian lens as relations of subject and subject-to), constitute the dynamic movement of the subjectifying operation of the new racial sensibility, read as dispositif. Shock implies a moment of shame in which a radical disorientation results from an excited and vertiginous self-awareness, resulting in a generative if chaotic moment of creativity. I also described a moment of capture in which this productivity is suppressed, snared and collapsed back into an all-consuming interiority. In the moment of flutter and in Whitey's confession, we see these two moments transposed one upon the other: we see the shame through which a unique exposure takes place, a shame concentrated on the very material being of the white body, but also the rationalization of that shame as it is absorbed into a form of speech that purports to reveal hidden things, to expose a something hidden deep inside. Whether through flutter or self-disclosure, shame's trauma is transmuted into talk and through talk into a very different emotion—guilt. Unruly shame is captured as it is mapped onto the stable terrain of an interiority that is being revealed through compulsive guilty speech. The aim of the present chapter is to consider the first moment of this racializing subjection, to explore the flux and the shock of shame and to trace the pattern of its dynamic movement. This effort will clear the way for the chapter that follows, which considers the capture of shame through its transmutation into guilt.

Toward this end, shame's generative force will be taken up in its social capacity as a profound experience of abandonment. The shamed subject, it will be argued, discovers himself suddenly alone as the world pulls away from what he has been exposed to be. As such, shame's abandonment can be traced to two characteristic scenarios: first in a scene of exposure before an Other, in which the rupturing of social bonds, particularly those mediated by shared relations of looking, or the interocular bond as Silvan Tomkins calls it, leaves the shamed subject stranded in painful isolation. Second, abandonment is played out in a fragmentation of the sense of contemporaneity, of a shared experience of time. The shamed subject, whose beholdency to some shaming attribute laid bare before the gaze of the Other, is a subject that lives stranded in a motionless time, the time of an unfree creature bound to what it is, in contrast to others who chose their futures freely. In both cases, abandonment through interocularity and through a split temporality makes it seem as if the shamed subject and his Other live on different planets, even as the trauma of this abandonment moves him to imagine new relations, both to the self and to the Other. This chapter will conclude a reflection on shame with a consideration of the powers of exposure and abandonment attributed to an Other thought to be capable of inducing such shame—a paranoid Other whose paranoia, I argue, brings a special capacity to see, to expose and to abandon, and whose presence saturates the contemporary racial field.

1 Exposure

Recent years have witnessed a surge of interest in the study of shame in the social sciences and in a number of related fields. Shame, it is argued, as a "master emotion," forms the general emotional and affective backdrop to much of contemporary social and personal life, although shame is often unacknowledged and circulates under a certain taboo (Scheff & Retzinger, 2001). Following the work of Thomas Scheff, shame is hailed as the archetypal social emotion. It serves an essential signal function for the individual, alerting her to the relative strength of the social bonds that sustain us, and to the normative proximity with those composing our social world. We feel shame when we are too close to other people—a moment of dependence or engulfment which accompanies experiences of public vulnerability, weakness, exposure and a failure to manifest sufficient autonomy. But we also experience shame when we are kept too far apart, when we are sanctioned or excluded from the normative boundaries of the community. Where fear signals to us of dangers posed to our physical safety, shame provides an equally vital warning of dangers to the social self, always under the threat of abandonment. In this sense, shame is the medium of social life itself, the emotion that embeds us in a network of ties and fields, that gives resonance to our feelings of being together with others. Yet the intensity and the dynamic character of the bond that shame enables remains under a veil, not only to others but to the shamed subject herself. Shame's dynamism, the relationality of the bond it sustains, necessarily subjects it to a certain prohibition, a taboo, particularly in English-speaking countries. Scheff describes how the German and French languages contain words for two different kinds of shame which are not acknowledged in English: everyday shame (scham and pudeur) and disgrace shame (schande and honte). That this distinction is absent in English reflects the unusually intense anxiety attending to the most mundane experiences of shame in English-speaking countries. Lacking a word for such everyday shame states, English language discussions have fostered an impenetrable taboo around all shames, proffering a broad set of oblique references that suppress any richer understanding of shame's dynamic, if sometimes toxic, social properties (Scheff, 2003, p. 241). So we don't refer to shame at all, preferring phrases such as "feel weird," "get flustered," "sense awkwardness," to direct expressions of shame—words many of us would readily apply to experiences with race. As such, shame's exclusion from the social field deprives us of an essential social capacity, a signal function that links us to others. Awareness of the threat of shame provokes us into certain caring relations with others as we seek to identify shame sources in others and in ourselves, and as we bend to protect and sensitize others to the shames that threaten us. In short, the withdrawal of shame from this social field signals the impoverishment of social bonds themselves, which are drained of a certain dynamic quality. To understand the odd ways in which white reracialization induces such intense feelings of shame, we have to grasp the social character of shame, and those relations by which shame emerges from a complex intersubjective dynamic, organized around a certain rhetoric of exposure.

Shame feelings are bound up with a sense of uncontrolled exposure before the judgment of an Other who gazes upon some aspect of oneself that one would prefer to keep hidden. In shame, we replay this exposure, replicating the Other's repudiation in our own self-regard (Tangney & Fischer, 1995; Tangney & Dearing, 2002; Lewis, 1992). Just as the Other disowns us, judges us, casts us out and turns away from us, so in shame we reproduce this operation on some part of our selves, disowning some aspect or feature that is suddenly disclosed to us as intolerable. Even when the Other doesn't directly see us, shame ignites as we picture what the Other would think if they did. Thus, it is possible to understand shame in terms of those ways of knowing that are made possible through interpersonal encounters, mediated by reciprocal acts of looking, although this reciprocity is far from stable. The relations of exposure that bring shame are of a certain kind: exposure, in contrast to reciprocal looking, implies an economy of looking that is skewed or disrupted, expressed not in a respectful regard so much as in a gawk or a stare. The shaming gaze is only half manifest, broken or halted, a gaze withdrawn and denied, an obscure gaze that can't bear to settle on its object and glances down or to the side rather than share itself with the Other. As only half given, the exposing gaze is one that cannot be precisely replicated within the shamed subject, or returned to the Other in a spirit of reciprocity. Shame is the interruption of a bond of intimacy and familiarity derived from mutual acts of looking, expressed in the reciprocal ocular bond. As that bond is broken and the shaming subject looks away, shame ensues. As Silvan Tomkins puts it: "the eyes not only can witness any affect in the face of the Other but also express one's own affect to the Other, and since this can be a shared experience, interocular intimacy becomes the occasion … of experiencing shame about any affect" (Tomkins, 1995, p. 147). In other words, shame only develops as that bond is broken, and as this gaze is withdrawn, reciprocated only as a distanced and absent gaze, the gaze of an intimate who has become an indifferent stranger. One has only to think of the social function of the eye-roll that interrupts a conversation to conjure the impression of this broken gaze.

Shameful exposure is a response to a furtive and imprecise look, a wince or a sudden downward glance, a gaze that is interrupted and abruptly withdrawn, and it is the instability of this gaze that lends to shame its uniquely traumatizing effect and that avails it to such powerful investments of fantasy and desire. The shamed subject extends out to the withdrawn gaze that has brought it such shame, pleading for exculpation and understanding, although this extension is always shaky and unstable, owing to the nonreciprocal nature of shame's diverted look. This is shame as a "broken circuit"—a theme developed by Lauren Berlant through her interpretation of Tomkins: shame is expressed by a break in the bond, mediated by mutual looking, between the individual and the desired affirmation of the community (Najafi et al., 2008). Tomkins puts it this way: "Shame is both an interruption and a further impediment to communication, which is itself communicated. When one hangs one's head or drops one's eyelids, or averts one's gaze, one has communicated one's shame and both the self and the face unwittingly become more visible, to the self and to others" (Tomkins, 1995, p. 137).

Exposure before a strange Other is a widely invoked theme in critical approaches to shame (Crozier, 2001; Lewis, 1998). Carl Schneider has described an etymological association that ties exposure to feelings of shame: to ex-pose is a derivation of the Latin *exponere*, meaning to put or to place out, which corresponds to contemporary meanings implying "to deprive of shelter," "to lay open" (Schneider, 1977, p. 34). Such a placing out, Schneider argues, implies a disruption of the proper place of (social) things: "Shame arises when something doesn't fit," or when one is placed out from the protective context provided by one's typical or preferred placement (35). In shame we are excluded, placed out from our niche in a community through the exposure and judgment of our private flaws—things which should have been kept hidden. Shame signals to others and to ourselves the need to protect what is vulnerable in us from the diminishment that would result as the consequence of such public placing. Schneider writes: "put simply, shame and blushing are meant to conceal, to cover that which is vulnerable to a perceived threat" (31). Colloquial references to the sexual organs and to the imperative of their concealment affirm this association of shame with exposure and protection, as with the phrase "shameful parts"—an association confirmed by Freud in his claim that the origins of shame in human evolution could be traced to man's emergence to an upright gait, which "made his genitals, that before had been covered, visible and in need of protection" (Freud, 1961, p. 46). Thus, as an effect of exposure, shame is less a moral than an ontological emotion. Shame touches on our somatic condition, corresponding less to the consequences of our behaviors than to the sense we develop of our very being—a sense that derives from epistemic sources, and from our general feeling of being known to others (Sartre, 1993; Levinas, 2003).

In exposure we are abandoned by the Other as the Other turns from us, aghast at what it has seen. We bury our face in our hands and curl our bodies, wishing to sink into ourselves and disappear. Yet, at the same time, this shrinking back from the exposing gaze is also a perverse yearning to renew such a bond, or possibly to enact it in a new way. In shame we seek to be invisible, but in making ourselves disappear, in covering our face we transmit to the Other a new or desperate presence. This is an ambivalence that Tomkins captures in the actions of the ashamed child who covers her face with her hand, yet peers through her fingers as if inviting some new contact: "Because the self is not altogether willing to renounce the object, excitement may break through and displace shame at any moment, but while shame is dominant it is experienced as an enforced renunciation of the object. Self-consciousness is heightened by virtue of the unwillingness of the self to renounce the object" (Tomkins, 1995, pp. 137–8). It is the movement of this excitement, the improvisatory gesture of shame's performativity toward the Other that differentiates shame's productivity from the passive suspension that one finds in guilt's judgment (Halperin & Trauss, 2010). Shame invites a moment of productive mourning for a lost

Other and a lost self. Or, as Elspeth Probyn puts it, shame occurs in "that little moment of disappointment—'oh, I was interested'" (Probyn, 2005, p. 13). And importantly, this performative gesture is intensified into a self-referential engagement in a moment that combines a gesture toward the Other with a renewed engagement with oneself. The persistence of this interest in the Other is central to the productive dynamic of shame which extends both outward and inward, both toward a new and different bond with the Other but also toward novel modes of self-discovery and self-formation. It would be a mistake to consider shame's persistence as a desire to appease or to return to an original interrupted intimacy. For Probyn, this means that the interest that is suspended yet not entirely diminished in shame becomes active in opening new fields of association: "interest is positive in its sense of being opposed to a negative or substrative state: it adds rather than takes away… it produces effects—more shame, more interest—which may be felt at a physiological, social or cultural level" (Probyn, 2005, p. 15). In this sense, shame can be understood as productive of new relations, as a making emotion.

We can trace the movement of white shame, and the ambivalent movement of shame's productive effect through an analogy with the blush (Crozier, 2001; Probyn, 2005; Bozalek et al., 2018). Like the raced body, the blush is something to which we are bound, yet something that interrupts the notion we hold of ourselves as sovereign creatures of public life. Like our races, our blushes are "ours," whether we like them or not: we all own our blushes, even if we wish we didn't. Even for those who have come to love their racial bodies as things of pride and for whom this pride has become a means of deflecting shame, just as for those for whom this body is a silent presence that allows them to cast shame on others from a place of invisibility, race is never entirely free of the potential for this blush (Nathanson, 1992, pp. 83–86). "Race is an idea, not a fact," Nell Irvin Painter notes, and in this sense the very idea of race is inflected with the sense of a helpless nudity before others, the exposure of a material, biological substrata subtending our civil identities, the very indecency of which can only be disguised through compensatory gestures of pride and respect, fumbling euphemisms, embarrassed agreement and shamed avoidance (Fredrickson, 2002; Painter, 2010, p. ix). Or, for those who have long enjoyed the privilege of a certain naturalness with regard to their race, who have come to think of themselves as beyond race and for whom the ebbing of that naturalness in recent years has left their bodies exposed as raced for the first time, race's blush brings a particularly toxic strangeness, a profound sense of helplessness and an ineluctable panic. The blush we have for this body, the body that is the effect of the very idea of race, is the body that embarrasses our pretenses to freedom. It is flesh in rebellion, a shameful body that is beyond our power to either control of conceal, or to abandon or escape. A woman, a compulsive blusher, tells the story of her encounter with a particularly handsome doctor whose good looks trigger a cycle that takes her from blush to blush-consciousness, to further blush—a cascading pattern that, once initiated proves impossible to contain. "I see blushing" she writes "as a loud-mouthed friend who insists on telling the world exactly what you're thinking, and worse, often explains it badly" (Townsend, 2016). In this way, racial subjection is like blushing, a generative, loud-mouthed affect that operates through the material sense of corporeal life.

Racial shame, like the blush, institutes a certain traumatic separation of the subject from others and from herself (Garlan, 1988). Shamed blushing, as a state of exposure before others, comes as the self is drawn up before the judgment of an Other whose gaze has special qualities which we cannot fully reproduce within ourselves, yet which we nonetheless invest and incorporate into the novelty of a certain self-discovery. Shame, or perhaps certain shames in certain ways, by exposing us to others also exposes us to ourselves, and in so doing moves us productively to a form of self-making. It is in this way that it is possible to find in shame a moment of autonomy that aligns with Foucault's discussion of subjection: shame is an other-related emotion, although this other-relatedness does not exhaust all the ways in which shame affects us. Shame comes through the Other, though ultimately it is an Other that abandons us to a painful autonomy (Benedict, 2005; Taylor, 1985; Tangney & Fischer, 1995). The ocular relations through which the Other sees into us and brings us to see into ourselves define the Other-related character of shame, though shame persists long after the Other has looked away, forgiven us or simply lost interest in the original offense. In other words, the Other serves as the trigger or the impetus for a set of affective responses that place the subject in an entirely personal relation to herself. In shame, the bond with the Other is severed and we are abandoned to ourselves, unbearably (Sartre, 1993, p. 284; Zahavi, 2014). As such, this shameful interiority, like the moment of the blush, is often experienced as a lonely thing. With the autonomy of this encounter comes a certain trauma, a sense of self made strange and frightful through its abandonment as the state of being to which we are condemned is experienced as a devouring monstrosity, something we long to escape (Lewis, 1971b, p. 41; Levinas, 2003). This encounter necessarily shakes us up, and in many ways freezes the subject in a state of inaction. Our sense of an unfolding future collapses as our freedom to shape that future appears reduced to what is already given in us, our transcendence crushed into our immanence, what we do reduced to what we are and will always be, and we are abandoned to an unbearable present from which no intentional action can originate. Shame's exile, and the autonomous relation to the self that it unfolds, comes with the collapse of this shared temporality that we enjoyed with the Other, wherein we are abandoned as a thing. As Lisa Guenther puts it: "Shame makes me feel frozen in time, stuck to a moment that goes nowhere," yet at the same time, she adds, shame can also "pull me out of myself, disrupting the complacency and self-satisfaction of the same" (Guenther, 2011, p. 25). This sense of the ambivalence of shameful abandonment, wherein we are frozen while being pulled out of ourselves, I would contend, represents the double character of shame expressed in many of those white racial moments described in the new racial sensibility.

The author Tim Wise has written extensively on whiteness and antiracist politics in a series of critical works and memoirs, variously pointing out the ways in which white people might think and engage differently with the racial order from which they derive unacknowledged benefits. In one conversation, Wise recalls a moment in which his own thoughts triggered in him a response that, I would contend, crystalize the effect of white shame. The author is boarding an airplane when he notices in the cockpit two African American pilots: "Sadly, my first thought was 'Oh god, can these two guys really fly this plane?'" Wise reports. "Just as quickly as that thought came into my head I was able to defeat it, I knew instantly that such a thought was absurd, but in that moment, I was beholden to my condition…" (Wise, 2013). This is a scene infused with shame. Wise's desire to abandon his own thoughts is one he arrives at through a duplication of the abandonment he imagines he would suffer should the pilots have had the opportunity to overhear them. But Wise's beholdency, and the very condition that generated these thoughts are not unique: Wise felt shame, one can speculate, not for an act he had committed, nor for the consequences of this act upon others, but for a "condition" that was revealed to himself about himself in the moment that those thoughts occurred: if nothing else, his thoughts remove him, not just from the social bonds that tied him to others, but from the expression of that bond in a shared sense of time. The time that binds him to the pilots is shattered, condemning him to a lonely time that extends back to his white racial condition, and forward only to his beholdency. As we explore the temporal structure of a shame that unfolds through the new racial sensibility, we come to understand more about this unique abandonment, but also about the autonomy and the productivity that this shame makes possible.

2 On the Other Side of Time

Just as the blush takes us out of social play, so in shame we experience the trauma of being outside of social time, a certain traumatic atemporality. Shame brings trauma, in the sense that trauma robs us of the possibility of moving on, of projecting a future or of possessing possibilities. Shame condemns us to repeat over and over an event, or a state of being, beyond which we cannot progress. In shameful exposure our story is already out there, already known to the one who sees through us, and sees into what we are. We are "beholden," as Wise put it, incapable of any movement that is not already written, already foretold by that awful thing we have been revealed to be and to which we feel ourselves bound (Nathanson, 1987). There is perhaps no more brutal demonstration of one's exposure before another than the expression of tired certainty with which the Other waits at the end of our story, knowing fully well what we're going to say and where things are headed. So exposed are one's motivations, so transparent one's thinking that anyone can tell at a glance all the possibilities that one might contain. It is for this reason that the Other looks away, not necessarily out of disgust or disapproval, but out of weariness for a story whose ending is already given at the very outset. Iteration of this tired certainty in the face of white rationalization is a hallmark of the new racial sensibility: "well intended" whiteness, bound as it is to a racial materiality of which it is scarcely aware and from which it cannot escape, tells only stories that are unbearably predictable. Such white testimonies have been heard a hundred times, their protests play out like overworn fables. Consider this sentence from DiAngelo's influential book: "Because of its seeming innocence, well-meaning white women crying in cross-racial interactions is one of the more pernicious enactments of white fragility" (133). I would imagine that it would be impossible for any white woman who has wept in the course of a discussion of race to read this sentence without feeling some trace of shame. Perhaps deservedly so. For DiAngelo, women moved to tears in racial conversations perceive themselves as "well-meaning," though their real potentials are transparent. Though these women don't realize it, their tears only monopolize the discussion, recentering the conversation around distressed whiteness in a ploy that is already obvious to others. These motivations are "pernicious," suggesting that there is an actor within oneself of which one is unaware, though which others gaze upon freely. The self one thinks of as "well-meaning," is one which someone else, a stranger, can clearly see is in fact motivated by more pernicious aims. DiAngelo goes on with her example:

> A black man who was struggling to express a point referred to himself as stupid. My co-facilitator, a black woman, gently countered that he was not stupid but that society would have him believe that he was. As she was explaining the power of internalized racism, a white woman interrupted with, "what he was trying to say was…" When my co-facilitator pointed out that the white woman had reinforced the racist idea that she could best speak for a black man, the woman erupted in tears. (133)

It is with an air of certainty that DiAngelo sees through this woman's tears to the very wellsprings of her motives, which remained veiled to the woman herself. "Tears that are driven by white guilt are self-indulgent. When we are mired in guilt, we are narcissistic and ineffective; guilt functions as an excuse for inaction" (DiAngelo 136). It is not difficult to read in this moment all the elements of a traumatic racial shame: through her interruption and DiAngelo's call out, the white woman found herself subjected to a painful exposure, her arrogance and entitlement laid bare before strangers who are quick to intuit her subordination to all she has inherited with her whiteness and even to her own white flesh, as well as the impossibility of her ever escaping the devouring gravity of this whiteness without some radical break in her identity. Yet with the sudden appearance of this hidden aspect before strangers there occurs an important element unique to the upsurge of shame's traumatic effect: the woman's captivity to a time that she cannot transcend is laid plain. She is alone in this time. While the time of others unfolds with decisions, actions and possibilities, her time is already told, her tears already determined with the predictability of a wound watch. Finding herself alone, a machine among humans, she panics, partly for the moral flaws and the "condition" that is exposed, but also, one might surmise, for the future that has been given away.

The colonization of the Other's time is something we all do. Anticipating the Other's actions is an activity that infiltrates those everyday acts of social typification through which we make our way through complex societies.

The colonization of futures through such acts of typing is inevitable, although through the lens of race this colonization takes on a uniquely toxic character. In a sense, race might be said to function as social information like any other, and as such can provide the basis for all kinds of predictive guesses, not unlike those we make on the basis of clothing, music or gait. Just ask any waiter or waitress and you'll learn the practical handicraft through which food and beverage choices can be predicted in advance on the basis of such visible social information as hair styles and accents. But you'll also learn of the need to conceal such typifying calculations, at the risk of causing deep offense. The insult of being known in advance on the basis of attributes of which one is not fully conscious is a feeling that invests the affective fields of racial sociability, and one to which the new racial sensibility has given a specific name. Derald Wing Sue's studies of "racial microaggressions" have had a tremendous influence on those literatures that compose the new racial sensibility, expanding from his initial publication of research on this topic in 2007 to a series of books, lectures and workshops that have drawn focused attention on verbal and interactive slights long conspicuous to people of color (Wing Sue et al., 2007). A microaggression reflects those "brief and commonplace daily verbal, behavioral, or environmental indignities, whether intentional or unintentional, that communicate hostile, derogatory, or negative racial slights and insults toward people of color" (271). The offense of a microaggression stems from the certainty with which it reduces the freedom of the Other, the future and the past of strangers, to the simple determinants of a condition of racial being revealed through a casual remark. When a person of color employed at a prestigious firm is asked, "how did you get your job," when an Asian American is complimented for speaking good English, or when a Latino American is asked where he comes from, these microaggressions, according to Wing Sue, convey specific messages: "People of color are given extra and unfair benefits because of their race" or "You are not American." Yet what is striking in these microaggressions is the shame that they impose, specifically through the temporalities they collapse. They presume to assess, not just the moral character of the individual, but the very potentials and futures this individual might possess. Microaggressions capture the vital movement of the Other within a scheme that ultimately confiscates that future, condemning them to a past from which they cannot escape. More insidiously, the collapsed future is tied directly to a past, a racial legacy and a genetic inheritance, to which the future is bound. The presence of our racial bodies traces us back to primordial origins, perhaps in family life, ethnic cultures or even through the biology of the species, while it consigns us to typified futures marked by preset tastes, capacities and aptitudes. Through the lens of racial typification, racial being confines one to what one has always been and will always be—a fusing of past and future in which the present is entirely disappeared. Such an atemporality is apparent in Fanon's account of being accosted in a Parisian train station: "Below the corporeal schema I had sketched out a historic-racial schema. The elements that I used had been provided for me by…the other, the white man, who had woven me out of a thousand details" (Fanon, 1967, p. 111). Embedded in every microaggression is a tiny shame, and within that shame a traumatic, lonely atemporality split off from others, a condemnation to a timeless present whose suffocating closure imposes its own moment of abandonment and panic.

We panic in shame for the future we have lost and for the reciprocity of the gaze that turns away. We panic for the helplessness this loss imposes and the abandonment it brings. But at the same time the loss of this temporal trajectory makes the frozen moment stand out in startling detail. Shame's atemporality and the isolation we feel before the broken gaze of the Other is one that heightens our awareness of things that had previously remained camouflaged by a certain familiarity. Panicked states are complex, and not always the best for clear thinking, but they are also moments in which the dulling effects of temporal routine give way to startling precision and even transformative epiphanies. Thus shamed, we become aware of things that had previously escaped our attention, and if the dread of what we have discovered is not all-consuming, inner qualities emerge with starting clarity. As Donald Nathanson writes:

> The very ability of shame affect to upset all mental activity, to afflict muscle tone in the head and the neck, to wrestle gaze away from what might have occupied us only a moment ago—all these powers of shame force us to consider who we were before shame hit and to what we have returned as shame subsides. Shame is the affect most likely to produce attention to the nature of the self. Shame produces a painful self-awareness at every stage in human development simply because of the ability of this affect script to interfere with every pleasant way we know ourselves. (Nathanson, 1992, p. 211)

Consider, for example that increasingly familiar rhetorical performance that is spread across the new racial sensibility, the white racial *mea culpa*, or public apology for the way in which it expresses white racial shame's thematization of self-awareness. Such apologies have been offered with such frequency by public figures in media and popular culture as to constitute a recognizable rhetorical pattern identified by conservatives as the "woke apology" (Lowry, 2021). Whether such apologies are sincere or not seems secondary to their phenomenological content, and to the precision with which they describe this moment of self-reflection, even if that moment disappears the instant it enters into the apology itself. I would like to examine two such apologies.

In 2020, *New York Times* food columnist Alison Roman apologized to cookbook author Chrissy Teigen and lifestyle consultant Marie Kondo after criticizing these women for various professional gaffes, which included the creation of product lines for Target or for insufficient content on their Instagram accounts. Her comments fed quickly into a series of Twitter exchanges where it was suggested that such comments directed by a white woman (Roman) to two Asian women constituted an instance of racial bias. Roman provided the following apology: "I need to formally apologize to Chrissy Teigen and Marie Kondo. I used their names disparagingly to try and distinguish myself, which I absolutely do not have an excuse for. It was stupid, careless and insensitive. I need to learn, and respect, the difference between being unfiltered and honest vs. uneducated and flippant." On the question of the racial character of her remarks, Roman wrote: "The fact that it didn't occur to me that I had singled out two Asian women is one hundred percent a function of my privilege (being blind to racial insensitivities is a discriminatory luxury). I know that our culture frequently goes after women, especially women of color, and I'm ashamed to have contributed to that" (Koenig, 2020).

Or, consider another apology, offered in 2022, by Columbia University psychiatrist Jeffrey Lieberman. In the Spring of that year, Lieberman tweeted his admiration for the Instagram celebrity and Sudanese-American model Nyakim Gatwech, a woman whose deep black skin hue has shaped her unique online celebrity and earned her the nickname "queen of the dark"—a term she has welcomed. In his tweet, Lieberman exclaimed at her beauty: "Whether a work of art or freak of nature she's a beautiful sight to behold." The phrase "freak of nature," possibly a reference to a rumor that her skin had been recognized by the *Guinness Book of World*

Records as the darkest human skin on record, quickly circulated on Twitter and Instagram, moving Lieberman to composed a public apology: "I tweeted from my personal account a message that was racist and sexist. Prejudices and stereotypical assumptions I didn't know I held have been exposed—to myself and you—, and I'm deeply ashamed and very sorry… An apology from me to the Black community, to women, and to all of you is not enough. I've hurt many, and I am beginning to understand the work ahead to make needed personal changes and overt time to regain your trust" (McWhorter, 2022).

Apologies are not themselves proof that any sincere shaming has occurred, and many of these apologies are dismissed out of hand by those to whom they are offered. But the recurrence of specific themes within these apologies suggests a certain continuity of experience across these panicked moments, and across experiences of white shame itself. Each apology speaks of a marked break in the subject's social trajectory, and of the discovery of a long concealed attribute suddenly brought to light by the offending incident and by the exposure that resulted. Each speaks of the sense of isolation from a wider community and of a commitment to self-transformation such a discovery imbibes, and each speaks of a new sense of self-transparency earned through the experience of shame. There is a sense in which, with shame's broken time and with the inner terrain it opens up, we are close to the relation of subjection as described by Foucault: exile from the regard of the Other ruptures the temporal bond, and delivers us over to a self that is opened up in shame. To claim that these shaming moments constitute all the things that Foucault said about the effect of subjection is perhaps going too far. Shaming, by itself, does not constitute the fully developed function of an acquired subjectivity, as Foucault put it, "tied to his own identity by conscience or self-knowledge" (Foucault, 1996, p. 331). But in contrast to that other moment, of becoming subject to the rule of another, there is much in shame that suggests a separate relation. In shame, we look within, unsettlingly, and with new eyes. We see something we didn't want to see, learn things we didn't want to learn, and in so doing we come to know ourselves differently. Affirmations that "I need to learn," or that aspects of myself that "I didn't know I held have been exposed—to myself and you," suggest that the derivation of this insight constitutes a profound and unsettling moment of self-reflection. It is in this sense that apology often implies, not just regret, but an odd sense of gratitude: we resent ourselves for the transgression that led to our abandonment and in a sense we abandon ourselves in turn, but we are also glad for having been afforded the opportunity to reflect on ourselves, and even to pursue the possibility of change.

3 A Paranoid Episteme

Guidetoallyship.com is a popular website distributing materials related to social justice and racial equity activism. Among its contents, it includes a feature on white allyship that offers a set of clear-cut rules to guide the public behavior of whites seeking to adopt appropriate behavior in the company of people of color. Under a heading, "What does it mean to be a white ally?" the following requirements are posted: "To Be An Ally Is To… Take on the struggle as your own; Transfer the benefits of your privilege to those who lack it; Amplify voices of the oppressed before your own; Acknowledge that even though you feel pain, the conversation is not about you; Stand up, even when you feel scared; Own your mistakes and de-center yourself; Understand that your education is up to you and no one else" (Guidetoallyship.com, 2021). What is offered here is an emotional script designed to make it possible for whites and people of color to work together, and to prevent certain white dispositions from impinging on the time and dignity of their black colleagues. But there is also a deep sense in which the rules are being issued by one who knows the secret reason that white people tend do these things, who sees and knows something about the white subject which the white subject does not yet know. Though it is not stated, it is implied strongly that some moment of exposure has already taken place, and that some truth about the white subject has already been learned by another. In this respect, this statement and statements like it function as therapeutic diagnoses, albeit ones performed by a therapist who is only reluctantly drafted into this operation. A section on how to "own your own mistakes" demonstrates the force of this exposure:

> You may have noticed it's easier to handle being corrected about something you didn't know if you're grateful for and even open to the opportunity to learn rather than embarrassed to have been wrong. Being able to let go of your ego is an incredibly important skill to develop. Try starting with "Thanks for letting me know" to put yourself in a better frame of mind. If

after you say that, you need to take some time to think about the situation, that's fine, too.

Feelings of "embarrassment" imply an Other before whom one is exposed, and who sees into oneself and turns away. This implies a degradation that can be avoided only if one identifies with and invests this withdrawn gaze, if one takes this gaze into oneself and begins to reassess oneself from its vantage point. In so doing, it is thought, one derives a certain distance on oneself, confining one's debasement to a part that suffers defilement while another part, in effect, administers this defilement, while looking on from a distance. Such emotional scripts represent, without a doubt, a productive and necessary step in the learning of behaviors required for more egalitarian civilities. Their unique strength lies in their prioritization of the interactive needs of those who bear the brunt of white racism over the psychic needs of white subjects themselves. But also, as I have already suggested, by softening the humiliation of white exposure through such an identification with the exposing perspective, they imply that some exposure has already taken place, and that such exposure is perhaps already an inevitable fact of all racialized interactions. Iterations of this exposing rebuke appear across the conversation of the new racial sensibility, often taking on a recognizably sardonic tone, as implied by the title of the Netflix series "Dear White People," for example, or in an article that appeared in *Forbes Magazine* in the summer of 2020, which offers "5 Uncomfortable Truths Black Colleagues Need You To Know." The article include Truth #2—Even if you personally haven't offended anyone (that you know of), you may indeed be part of the problem, and Truth #3—Every black person on your team is not your "friend." In all these instances, white people derive a sense of being somehow already known. They presume a standpoint from which whiteness is already laid bare, its secrets exposed, but that this standpoint is necessarily one that will always elude white comprehension itself, fragmented and withdrawn as it may be (Brownlee, 2020).

In this chapter I have tried to explain those moments of shamed exposure that accompany the new racial sensibility, and how those moments induce a certain unsettling reflection in which the subject develops some new relation to itself in which taken-for-granted aspects emerge as suddenly strange, new and unsettling. I have tried to describe the panicked responses of this subject, and how, with the onset of shame and in a moment of suspended temporality, this subject is nudged to enact a new time, a new relation to its own being and to the social fields through which shame develops. This is the shamed productivity that, I have argued, cuts new paths and enacts new possibilities, and in so doing gums up the gears of the racial order by subverting those processes of white racial subjection that are so important to its functioning. Although, as we shall see in the next chapter, this productivity is restrained and absorbed into the stable interior forms of the guilty white subject. But before leaving the discussion of this shame, I would like to give a little more detail to an important function of this exposing and abandoning moment, one which pertains to the social field from which shame develops and to the epistemic character of that gaze brought to bear by an Other who sees so much and induces such panic. How is it imagined that this Other, as a racial Other, might possess some faculty capable of such a unique penetration into the most enigmatic folds of the white racial secret? What is the character of this special knowledge that the Other is presumed to possess, and how is it equipped with such a devastating capacity to convey such abandonment?

The exposure of whiteness from which shame feelings derive takes place against the backdrop of a complex set of arrangements that determine who can produce knowledge about whom and how that knowledge is validated, and by implication, who is in a position to expose whom and thus to cast shame. A golden rule of the new racial sensibility maintains the impossibility of truly knowing or speaking for another's racial experiences—a rule that applies to all racial groups except for whites, for whom the reverse is true. Whites can never fully know even their own racial experience (although some come closer than others), the contents of which are widely and readily available only to adjacent, or subaltern racial groups. That white people must know, but can never truly know what others already know about them is an organizing assumption of the new racial sensibility extending to its origins as a vernacular form. This view has long circulated among black authors, reflected in a statement by James Weldon Johnson: "I believe it to be a fact that the colored people of this country know and understand the white people better than the white people know and understand them" (cited in Mills, 2007, p. 17). Thus, white self-knowledge can only come through some engagement with the knowledges of the social groups that surround it—subordinated groups imagined to be oracles of the white soul who already know white secrets better than whites ever can, but are wont to pass on this knowledge too casually for the fatigue and exhaustion such sharing necessarily brings. This sentiment is captured in Audrey Lorde's protest: "Black and Third World people are expected to educate white people as to our humanity," an expectation that, for people of color, implies an appropriation of black labor such as one might find under colonial or slave conditions, although this time it is a labor of a less menial, more therapeutic nature (Lorde, 1984, p. 115). Such reluctance, in white eyes, only inflates and confirms the certainty of the Other's oracular authority, and the exposures of which it is capable.

Such knowing must be understood in terms of the broader ethos that it unfolds, which views all knowledge as inextricably bound with struggle—a sentiment crystallized by Ibram Kendi's claim that "there is no such thing as a non-racist idea, only racist ideas and antiracist ideas" (Kendi, 2018). All knowledge, in this sense, functions as military intelligence in a world populated with enemies, some of whom reside in plain sight, others behind screens of deception and concealment, even the most genial of expressions. In this spirit, the new racial sensibility operationalizes a systemic distrust of surfaces as it valorizes special capacities for perception and decipherment. White conduct in racialized social interaction is a veil to be pulled back, a screen to be penetrated but also a hieroglyph to be studied and interpreted for the hidden meanings it might betray. The hermeneutic task which the new racial sensibility promotes is one that mobilizes a sixth sense, a supra-sensory intuition capable of detecting the hidden movements and truths that operate beneath the surfaces of interactive pleasantries. This work involves the fostering of these intuitive skills for the study of other's behaviors, though they can also be directed inward toward one's own thoughts, feelings and habits. The moment of subjection comes as the white subject undertakes to replicate this suspicious regard that she feels has been brought to bear on her and to apply the work of this decipherment in her own self-examination, although the replication of this hermeneutic gaze is inevitably partial and imperfect, owing to the ultimate inaccessibility of this knowledge itself.

Such a racial sixth sense shares some important features with the paranoiac, although I must add that such paranoia should not be reduced to the delusional or the psychotic. As Sarah Ahmed points out, sometimes there are grounds for racial paranoias, and the supra-sensory, enhanced perceptual capacities of the paranoid view often prove warranted by real social threats that are, as the paranoiac well knows, concealed. "Racism creates paranoia: that's what racism does. Racism is reproduced both by the fantasy of paranoia (it doesn't 'really' exist) and by the effect of the fantasy of paranoia, which is to make us paranoid" (Ahmed, 2009, p. 47). In fact, discussions of "cultural paranoia," "cultural mistrust" or the "healthy paranoia" adopted by African Americans as the inevitable cognitive defense made necessary by systemic racism has been a central theme of black psychology since the 1960s (Cobbs & Grier, 1968, p. 161; Sue et al., 2007, p. 332). Particularly where the object of fear is so diffuse and ephemeral, so slippery as to escape positive detection, an attitude of general paranoia is necessary as a strategy for psychic and sometimes physical survival (Yancy, 2008).

To put this differently, what is important here is not the veracity of paranoia in real life, but the logic it unfolds through its incorporation as a function of the new racial sensibility. Paranoia is, after all, contagious and replicates very quickly. The very promiscuity that this paranoid style implies and the ways in which paranoia lends itself, through the inventiveness that it licenses, to a range of appropriations and purposes, explains the epistemological character of the new racial sensibility, which is resolutely paranoid. The imperative of a certain paranoia is broadly inscribed across the discourse of this sensibility, just as it is in all those related professional fields from which it draws and which variously license its unique ways of knowing. In particular, with the new racial sensibility's professionalization of the paranoid stance, and with the shaping of this paranoia into a therapeutic program administered in a plurality of institutional contexts, paranoia becomes a general condition. As Freud suggested, paranoid sentiment operates through a range of scientific and theoretical fields, reflecting an "unpalatable external similarity and internal kinship to the systems of our philosophers" of which, by implication, the psychological sciences all share some part (Freud, 1919, p. 261, see also Sedgwick, 2003, p. 125). So, there is a sense in which we're all paranoid, or at least those of us who endeavor to describe and interpret the world. This is especially true of those of us who interpret the world out of a fear for their own survival, but also for those new therapeutic technologies that model themselves on this paranoia, and who apply the tools of modern therapeutic government to the task of regulating the behaviors of others by coming to know better their inner lives.

The "hermeneutics of suspicion" is a term applied to a long and deeply paranoid tradition of critical inquiry associated with Marx, Freud and Nietzsche, in which manifest representations are made to betray those hidden, less flattering truths they conceal—an unmasking tendency typically associated with overarching theories of power (Ricoeur, 2008, p. 32). To participate in the new racial sensibility is to practice the art of such an inquiry, though in so doing practitioners of this paranoid style evolve ways of knowing that are themselves uniquely active, that bring about specific effects in those upon whom they are brought to bear. Paranoid knowing models itself on the same devious and guileful quality that it seeks to expose. It is sneaky, combative knowledge that is well suited to an equally sneaky object, a special way of unmasking that cannot conform to the usual distancing posture that validates knowledge in more conventional contexts. What results is a function not unlike what Ian Hacking called "classificatory looping"—a co-production of anxious white subjects and the probing, paranoid discourses that threaten to poke through their white masks and expose their most private selves before a paranoid gaze (Hacking, 1995, p. 21). Paranoia produces those things of which one should be afraid: it unfolds more than what it sees and more than the things it exposes, and displays a spry capacity for the absorption of all critique as instance of a dangerous and cunning enemy intrusion. It composes a milieu all its own, or what Robert Jay Lifton terms a "sacred science" which combatively deflects experiences incompatible with its doctrinal stance as themselves *de facto* affirmations of the urgency and validity of doctrine itself: "any thought or action which questions the higher purpose is considered to be stimulated by a lower purpose, to be backward, selfish, and petty in the face of the great, overriding mission" (Lifton 422, 427). Just as criticism of Church orthodoxy only confirms the abomination of heresy or the refusal to admit to Oedipal urges only gives certainty to the diagnosis of "denial," so criticism of the new racial sensibility's paranoia is itself greeted as evidence of precisely the kind of white defensiveness this sensibility so urgently seeks to expose—a criticism from which, no doubt, these very pages will not be exempted. Eve Sedgewick reflects on the paranoid style implied by a hermeneutic of suspicion which, she argues, doubles itself as it comes to mimic the craftiness and stealth of the objects of its exposure: "Simply put, paranoia tends to be contagious; more specifically, paranoia is drawn toward and tends to construct symmetrical relations, in particular, symmetrical epistemologies," a point she clarifies in a citation from Leo Bersani: "Paranoia is an inescapable interpretive doubling of presence" (Sedgwick, 2003, p. 126). To the extent, then, that we look upon ourselves through a paranoid lens, we tend to produce within ourselves the kind of worlds that paranoia envisions—the cunning and guileful, but also the mysterious and enigmatic objects of which paranoia dreams. In this way, the new racial sensibility, as rogue, struggling, paranoid knowing that has to fight for its own existence in a world of enemies, together with the white subject who uncovers through this paranoia new and unsettling depths, unfolds the image of a

Hobbesian world within, an internal barbarism which emerges as an effect of its own nasty and brutish methods of exposure. The white subject, through this paranoid lens, encounters himself as a monster: a strange and violent creature whose barbarity unsettles all the assumptions of civility which she had been raised up to believe. It is a world in which force goes against force and any pretense to neutrality is greeted as further evidence of the deceitful hand. In fact, the more strident the appeals of the white subject to innocence, the more alert the paranoid gaze becomes to the sonorous stirrings of white privilege behind declarations of virtue. This is a view that has specific implications for racial liberalism, with its protestations of white innocence. Ta-Nehisi Coates, cautioning his son on the inevitable racism of educational institutions, puts it this way: "it does not matter that the 'intentions' of individual educators are noble. Forget about intentions. What any institution, or its agents, 'intend' for you is secondary. Our world is physical. Learn to play defense—ignore the head and keep your eyes on the body… 'Good intention' is a hall pass through history" (Coates, 2015, p. 33). In such a world, virtue is itself only another force—a rationale that gives no quarter to the virtuous.

The contagiousness of cultural paranoia, it seems to me, informs the new racial sensibility's imperative to expose the material forces operating behind the façade of civility, and thus to shame, but also to subject—to present the subject to itself as an enticing and impossible enigma. The white subject, as a fearful puzzle with pieces missing, is drawn into a certain inwardness and self-reflection. Paranoia, thus appropriated as a mode of truth production, is nothing if not exposing: it sees more than any mask can ever hide, and trains itself on spoiled motives. Paranoia is central to the new racial sensibility, though in an inverted sort of way. Through a process of appropriation and incorporation, paranoias like those described by Ahmed and Coates are made to assume a very deliberate set of functions quite remote from those described by these authors. With the expansion of the new racial sensibility, the kind of "healthy" paranoia long practiced on the racial margins and in those vernacular racial knowledges from which the new racial sensibility was culled, has been taken up, mirrored, codified and replicated in a discourse through which white people are brought to interrogate their own racial habits and sensibilities in a paranoid spirit. In this regard, paranoia has assumed a double function, first as resistant knowledge, as a means of preserving black life and second, through a process of appropriation and mimicry, as regulative knowledge, as a lens through which whiteness becomes racial, interrogates itself, seeks to decipher its signs, to undo the ruse of its own universality and to tease out its own hidden truths. It is this second life of paranoia, and not the first, that composes the lens through which whiteness, glimpsing itself and its inner life, enters into such a panic. The paranoid gaze, thus appropriated and internalized, gestures toward an omniscience that always sees and exposes so much more, and it is in this way that paranoia and shame fold so perfectly into subjection. Because paranoia itself is the irreducible property of the paranoid and can never be fully replicated, the paranoid gaze imposes an exposure that has no precise limits. Paranoia is never reciprocal: one has it, but never in a way that might be shared, like a friendly glance or a gaze of mutual acknowledgment. Paranoia is always broken, withdrawn, abandoning. It initiates a mystery, but also a deep and unsettling danger (Lindsay-Hartz, 1984). In this way, shame's exposure before the paranoid gaze brings a satiating epistemic dread: the white subject is convinced of her total exposure before a paranoid gaze she can never reproduce, her total transparency before a gaze that cannot be reciprocated or fully replicated, that is already a gaze broken off and withdrawn.

Jack Katz, in his discussion of shame as a social relation, describes the experience of an "eerie revelation" implied by a shameful exposure before an Other who knows. This eerie truth functions as what he terms an "abiding mystery, a personally relevant something-that-has-been-kept-hidden" (Katz, 1997, p. 235). "What is revealed to oneself in shame, as Adam and Eve discovered, is an omniscience about oneself that only the other can possess" (236). Where paranoid knowing envisions monsters, white racial subjection, in an attempt to mimic that paranoia, inscribes monstrosity deeply within the folds of its inner life, and recoils in panic. And to contain this panic, the white subject starts about the work of describing and interpreting, measuring and making amends for these monstrous rampages. As monstrous, this monstrous place can only be a place of dread and suffering, a shameful place one conspires to escape, through flutter or talk, as Whitey so desperately longs to do. The reflective knowledge we gain from this encounter is ignited by, but also remains captive to a paranoia which forecloses in advance any possibility of transcendence: it remains a knowledge which we can never fully possess. As such, it is this doubling of the paranoid gaze of the Other as a therapeutic mode of self-interrogation that constitutes the epistemic character of the white racial dispositif, a paranoid way of knowing that brings shame and abandonment, and induces the effects of white subjection.

4 The Master of Racial Truth

I have tried to describe the effects of white shame in such a way as to make clear their convergence in wider processes of racial subjection, and the derivation of a certain knowledge for which one feels shame. Subjection implies the capacity for self-knowledge, while in shame we know, or think we know, something about what the Other has come to know about us. In shameful exposure we attempt to replicate, however imperfectly, the Other's knowledge in our own self-understanding. Through this knowing we find ourselves set apart from others, abandoned and alone with ourselves, peering into what we are revealed to be with great apprehension. We want to know what the Other knows, so we take a deeper look into ourselves, subjecting time-worn habits to a new scrutiny. Through this paranoid gaze, biographies that long provided assurance and comfort are revealed as false and strange fictions that have to be revised as specifically white biographies; our best attributes have to be reconceived as white attributes, assets gleaned through a system of racial privilege. Everything that once gave comfort and security suddenly emerges as strange and hideous, like uncanny figures in a fun-house mirror, objects of violent struggle bringing convulsive shame. But the Other's paranoid gaze is hazy and indistinct, broken and withdrawn, the contents of its knowing remote and inaccessible owing to the special status of the Other's perspective. The Other turns away, denying the possibility of reciprocity, averting her eyes so as to hide her response to what she has observed, or perhaps the Other stands in a special place or occupies a special status that makes this knowledge unique, impossible to replicate. So, in shamed subjection, as in paranoia, we strive for a knowledge that we cannot attain and whose gaps we are forced to fill in with our imaginations—a condition which only makes us scrutinize ourselves with greater intensity and distress.

In short, this shaming effect folds neatly into the subjectifying function of the dispositif, and specifically through the therapeutic discourse of the new racial sensibility. Through subjection, expert knowledges operate across a certain interval, or through a division of labor that separates the expert from the laity. The expert's knowledge is of a different kind, held apart and qualified, invested with authority and mediated through a unique sagacity. It is through this interval that expert knowledge resonates with us in a certain way. The doctor pauses to think as he pokes at our skin or the therapist jots something down in her notepad, the contents of which we know we are not qualified to fully understand, yet whose inaccessibility incites us to imagine. He's thinking that those blemishes are cancerous, or she senses the neurotic pattern of my worrying! Whether this distance is racial or professional, or perhaps some combination of the two, the authority to decipher signs reigns down on a subject whose behavior or speech is made to signify. *Scientia sexualis*, as Foucault describes it, extracts a truth that is "present but incomplete, blind to itself, in the one who spoke [but] could only reach completion in the one who assimilated and recorded it... the master of truth" (Foucault, 1984, pp. 66–67). Though Foucault would probably not have made this characterization, it is easy to read the incompleteness that one experiences before a master of truth as an exposure before a partial, withdrawn gaze, a sense of visibility infused with feelings of shame. Blindness to oneself linked with a transparency before an Other brings an exposure before an authority who commands certain epistemic privileges and whose regard brings shame and subjection, or subjection through shame.

So the question then becomes: if we are to transpose this effect of shaming-subjection from the discourse on sexuality (where Foucault developed it) to the optics of racial affect (where I have attempted to apply it), then we might ask the question; how is this "master of truth" sustained as a mode of racial knowing? How is the interval or the gap through which this mastery of truth is inscribed with the power to decipher, and through which incompleteness in the one studied finds its completion in the master's gaze—how is this interval sustained as a uniquely racial interval, one characterized by a certain power to impose a uniquely racial shame? My answer, which I have tried to provide in this chapter, is that this epistemic distance as a mastery of racial truth is coded in those many popular, professional and institutional manifestations of the new racial sensibility as a therapeutic program, such as those we find in cultural competency training, diversity workshops and anti-racist self-help literatures. In these instances, unique ways of knowing are fashioned from the protocols and expert iterations of psychological knowledge, wherein the knower is set apart from the known. At the same time, in some undeclared way and drawing on those very structures of racial alterity that are already deeply inscribed within the white racial imaginary, the setting apart of this knowledge as the realm of a unique racial omniscience is an act that invests the racial Other with a certain power to see through, to expose, and thus to shame. In other words, the gaze that exposes whiteness is conflated with an expert gaze, the gaze of a therapeutic (if somewhat paranoid) professional, and through this curious transposition blackness is fixed in the mode of a certain professional mastery of white truth.

But this is not the only way that this scenario can play out. In the face of this operation, there are avenues through which this shame and this subjection might be practiced differently. Perhaps the work of a different kind of shameful white subjection might begin with the diminishment of the strangeness and the eerie quality through which a deep white panic is ignited. Perhaps this work might begin with a divestment of that paranoid knowing lavished on the Other, and with a setting aside of the omniscience with which the Other's knowledge is invested in the new racial sensibility and in all those institutional forms through which it is administered. If white subjects could stop freaking out and learn to view themselves as less strange, less frightening and less shameful, they might discover the productivity of their shame and direct it toward the work of an anti-racist white racial subjection. This is a subjection that might be carried out not in the technical space of an fictitious interiority, but through a lived emeddedness with the Other, in a shared social world and through real and shared social shames. This is a goal to which Robin DiAngelo at times seems to direct her readers, distinguishing as she does between racism as a deeply corrupted moral condition and racism as an inherited state: "I'm not saying you are immoral," she writes, as if to quiet the racial panic that so affects her readers, and to give them the focus they need to confront and modify their white habits without being overpowered by its shame (13). Indeed, DiAngelo provides a specific technique through which shame feelings might be dissipated in order that more practical anti-racist objectives might be pursued: "To interrupt white fragility, we need to build our capacity to sustain the discomfort of not knowing, the discomfort of being racially unmoored, the discomfort of racial humility" (14). However, her efforts are, in my reading, fraught with troubles, as the de-shaming she prescribes inevitably falls back into a reinvestment in the paranoia through which a certain shame becomes inevitable. And that is, perhaps, the wider function, if not of her personal intentions then of the genre within which she writes. The escape she offers from shame leads not to the development of shame's productive potential as a medium of renewal, but to the suppression, concealment or bypassing of shame through its transmutation into a technical program that suspends the white subject as the sustaining object of an ongoing interrogation. DiAngelo doesn't propose that we move beyond shame, only that we tolerate it and direct it toward more pragmatic ends. This is, as I have argued, a mode of transmutation through which shame is reexperienced as guilt, and as such constitutes a certain function whereby the indeterminacy of becoming a subject is ensnared, caught or arrested in a relation of being subject-to. It is to this process of the transmutation of shame into guilt, as the defining function of the new racial sensibility, that we now turn.

References

Ahmed, S. (2009, March). Embodying Diversity: Problems and Paradoxes for Black Feminists. *Race Ethnicity and Education, 12*(1), 41–52.

Alcoff, L. M. (2015). *The Future of Whiteness.* Polity Press.

Bailey, A. (2015). White Talk as a Barrier to Understanding the Problem of Whiteness. In G. Yancy (Ed.), *White Self-Criticality beyond Anti-racism: How Does It Feel to Be a White Problem?* Lexington Books.

Bailey, A. (2021). *The Weight of Whiteness: A Feminist Engagement with Privilege, Race and Ignorance.* Lexington Books.

Benedict, R. (2005). *Chrysanthemum and the Sword: Patterns of Japanese Culture.* Houghton Mifflin.

Bernasconi, R. (2001). Who Invented the Concept of Race? Kant's Role in the Enlightenment Construction of Race? In R. Bernasconi (Ed.), *Race.* Blackwell.

Bernasconi, R., & Lott, T. (2000). *The Idea of Race.* Hackett Publishing Company.

Bouson, B. J. (2000). *Quiet as it's Kept: Shame, Race and Trauma in the Novels of Tony Morrison.* SUNY Press.

Bozalek, V., Shefer, T., Carolissen, R., & Probyn, E. (2018). Productive Faces of Shame: An Interview with Elspeth Probyn. *Feminism and Psychology, 29*(2), 322–334.

Brownlee, D. (2020, June 16). Dear White People: Here Are 5 Uncomfortable Truths Black Colleagues Need You To Know. *Forbes.* Retrieved June 12 2023, from https://www.forbes.com/sites/danabrownlee/2020/06/16/dear-white-people-here-are-5-uncomfortable-truths-black-colleagues-need-you-to-know/?sh=137e80c0624e

Coates, T.-N. (2015). *Between the World and Me.* Speigel & Grau.

Cobbs, P. M., & Grier, W. H. (1968). *Black Rage.* Basic Books.

Crozier, R. W. (2001). Blushing and the Exposed Self: Darwin Revisited. *Journal for the Theory of Social Behavior, 31*(1), 61-72.

DiAngelo, R. (2018). *White Fragility: Why It's So Hard For White People To Talk About Racism.* Beacon Press.

Dolezol, L. (2016). *The Body in Shame: Phenomenology, Feminism and the Socially Shaped Body.* Lexington Press.

DuBois, W. E. B. (1994). *The Souls of Black Folk.* Gramercy Books.

Eddo-Lodge, R. (2017). *Why I'm No Longer Talking to White People about Race.* Bloomsbury.

Fanon, F. (1967). *Black Skin, White Masks* (C. L. Markmann, Trans.). New York: Grove Press.

Foucault, M. (1984). *The History of Sexuality, Volume 1, An Introduction* (R. Hurley, Trans.). Vintage Books.
Foucault, M. (1996). The Subject and Power. In J. D. Faubion (Ed.), *Michel Foucault: Power* (R. Hurley & Others, Trans.). The New Press.
Fredrickson, G. M. (2002). *Racism: A Short History*. Princeton University Press.
Freud, S. (1931). Preface to Reik's Ritual: Psycho-Analytic Studies. *Standard Edition of the Complete Psychological Works of Sigmund Freud, XVII*, (Trans. D. Bryan.) Hogarth Press 257–264.
Freud, S. (1961). *Civilization and its Discontents* (J. Strachey, Trans.). Norton.
Garlan, C. (1988). *Thinking about Trauma*. Routledge.
Guenther, L. (2011). Shame and the Temporality of Social Life. *Continental Philosophy Review, 44*(1), 23–39.
Guidetoallyship.com. (2021). Retrieved June 12 2023, from https://guidetoallyship.com.
Hacking, I. (1995). The Looping Effects of Human Kinds. In D. Sperber, D. Premack, & A. J. Premack (Eds.), *Causal Cognition: A Multidisciplinary Debate*. Oxford University Press.
Halperin, D., & Trauss, V. (Eds.). (2010). *Gay Shame*. University of Chicago Press.
Katz, J. (1997). The Elements of Shame. In M. R. Lansky & A. P. Morrison (Eds.), *The Widening Scope of Shame*. Analytic Press.
Kendi, I. X. (2018, January 13). The Heartbeat of Racism is Denial. *New York Times*. Retrieved June 12 2023, from https://www.nytimes.com/2018/01/13/opinion/sunday/heartbeat-of-racism-denial.html
Koenig, R. (2020, May 9). Alison Roman Apologizes Again to Chrissy Teigen for her 'Tone Deaf Remarks'. *Today*. Retrieved June 12 2023, from https://www.today.com/food/alison-roman-apologizes-chrissy-teigen-interview-diss-t181197
Levinas, E. (2003). *On Escape* (J. Rolland, Ed., and B. Bergo, Trans.). Stanford University Press.
Lewis, H. B. (1971b). *Shame and Guilt in Neurosis*. International Universities Press.
Lewis, M. (1992). *Shame: The Exposed Self*. Free Press.
Lewis, M. (1998). Shame and Stigma. In P. Gilbert & B. Andrews (Eds.), *Shame: Interpersonal Behavior, Psychopathology, and Culture*. Oxford University Press.
Lindsay-Hartz, J. (1984). Contrasting Feelings of Shame and Guilt. *American Behavioral Scientist, 27*, 689–704.
Lorde, A. (1984). *Sister Outsider: Essays and Speeches*. The Crossing Press.
Lowry, R. (2021, February 8). The Humiliating Art of the Woke Apology. *National Review*. Retrieved June 12 2023, from https://www.nationalreview.com/corner/the-humiliating-art-of-the-woke-apology/
McIntyre, A. (1997). *Making Meaning of Whiteness: Exploring Racial Identities with White Teachers*. SUNY Press.

McWhorter, J. (2022, March 1). One Graceless Tweet Doesn't Warrant Cancellation. *New York Times*. Retrieved June 12 2023, from https://www.nytimes.com/2022/03/01/opinion/psychiatry-professor-tweet.html
Mills, C. (2007). White Ignorance. In S. Sullivan & N. Tuana (Eds.), *Race and Epistemologies of Ignorance*. SUNY Press.
Mills, C. (1999). *The Racial Contract*. Cornell University Press.
Najafi, S., Serlin, D., & Berlant, L. (2008, Fall). The Broken Circuit: An Interview with Lauren Berlant. *Cabinet*, (31). Retrieved June 12 2023, from http://www.cabinetmagazine.org/issues/31/najafi_serlin.php
Nathanson, D. (1987). A Timetable for Shame. In D. Nathanson (Ed.), *The Many Faces of Shame*. The Guilford Press.
Nathanson, Donald L. (1992) *Shame and Pride; Affect, Sex and the Birth of the Self*. Norton
Painter, N. I. (2010). *The History of White People*. Norton & Co..
Probyn, E. (2005). *Blush: Faces of Shame*. University of Minnesota Press.
Ricoeur, P. (2008). *Freud and Philosophy: An Essay on Interpretation* (D. Savage, Trans.). Yale University Press.
Sartre, J. P. (1993). *Being and Nothingness* (H. E. Barnes, Trans.), original edition. Washington Square Press.
Schefer, T., & Munt, S. R. (2019). A Feminist Politics of Shame: Shame and its Contested Possibilities. *Feminism & Psychology, 29*(2), 145–156.
Scheff, T. (2003). Shame in Self and Society. *Symbolic Interaction, 26*(2), 239–262.
Scheff, T., & Retzinger, S. (2001). Shame as the Master Emotion of Everyday Life. *Journal of Mundane Behavior, 1*(3), 303–324.
Schneider, C. (1977). *Shame, Exposure and Privacy*. Norton.
Sedgwick, E. K. (2003). Paranoid Reading, Reparative Reading. In *Touching Feeling*. Duke University Press.
Strayed, C., & Almond, S. (2018). How Can I Cure My White Guilt? *New York Times*. Retrieved June 12 2023, from https://www.nytimes.com/2018/08/14/style/white-guilt-privilege.html
Sue, D. W., Capodilupo, C. M., Torino, G. C., Bucceri, J. M., Holder, A. M. B., Nadal, K. L., & Esquilin, M. (2007, May–June). Racial Microaggressions in Everyday Life: Implications for Clinical Practice. *American Psychologist, 62*(4), 271–286.
Tangney, J. P., & Dearing, R. L. (2002). *Shame and Guilt*. Guilford Press.
Tangney, J. P., & Fischer, K. (Eds.). (1995). *Self-conscious Emotions: the Psychology of Shame, Guilt, Embarrassment and Pride*. Guildford Press.
Taylor, G. (1985). *Pride, Shame and Guilt: Emotions of Self-assessment*. Clarendon.
Tomkins, S. (1995). Shame-Humiliation and Contempt-Disgust. In E. K. Sedgwick & A. Frank (Eds.), *Shame and its Sisters: A Silvan Tomkins Reader*. Duke University Press.

Townsend, K. (2016, June 30). Why Do People Blush? *The Atlantic*. Retrieved June 12 2023, from https://www.theatlantic.com/health/archive/2016/06/why-do-people-blush/489572/

Wise, T. (2013). *White Like* Me, documentary. Media Education Foundation. Retrieved June 12 2023, from https://www.youtube.com/watch?v=i58pG0pKHWY

Yancy, G. (2008). Elevators, Social Spaces and Racism: A Philosophical Analysis. *Philosophy & Social Criticism, 34 (*8). 843-876

Yancy, G. (2012). *Look, A White!: Philosophical Essays on Whiteness*. Temple University Press.

Zahavi, D. (2014). *Self and Other: Exploring Subjectivity, Empathy and Shame*. Oxford University Press.

CHAPTER 4

Guilt's Capture

Abstract In the face of novel forms of subjectivity introduced by the experience of shame, an accompanying function of the new racial sensibility seeks to transpose that novelty into a more readily managed emotional reaction. Through its appeal to a white interiority and by way of its therapeutic mandate, the new racial sensibility transmutes this disruptive shame into feelings of guilt in a function that reinscribes white subjectivity, suppressing its novelty and essentially conserving the white racial order from which this subjectivity develops. This process is described through a set of operations in which the white subject projects a certain mode of therapeutic authority onto the racial Other, who is presumed to know this white interiority in a therapeutic light.

Keywords Guilt • Projection • Transmutation • Psychoanalysis • Helen Lewis • Therapeutic ethos

Herbert Morris, an American philosopher and legal theorist who wrote broadly on the emotions in relation to moral life, provides a discussion of the contrasting ways in which shame and guilt stand before law. A child hits a playmate, Morris tells us, and is admonished for having done a bad thing, for which he will be punished if he does it again (Morris, 1976, pp. 60–63). You're a bad boy, he is told—a sanction that leads the child to discover the notion of a rule and to experience the feeling of guilt for

S. Binkley, *Against White Interiority*,
https://doi.org/10.1007/978-3-031-31828-3_4

having transgressed the rule and gotten caught. In this way, the state of guilt forms the basis of the subject of law (60). However, it is also possible that the scene might unfold differently: the parent says to the child: "that is what an animal does, not a human being," and turns away from the child in anger and distain. Under these conditions, the effect on the child is quite different. The child's self-awareness develops not through a relation of responsibility before the law but from a feeling of shame relative to a failed model identity, or a state of existence (being human) to which the child, by the fact of his very being, has failed to attain. In other words, guilt can be understood as a legalistic notion which addresses the consequences of our actions on others, while shame reflects an ontological preoccupation with the very character of our being relative to an ideal (62).

Morris explores the differences between these two outlooks in a series of comparative statements that are worth recalling: shame's sanction derives from its measurement against a perfect state ("that is what a pig would do!") and not obedience to a rule, registered through the judgment of another. Shame is therefore a scale morality (how closely do you resemble a pig?) which operates without clear boundaries, while guilt is a threshold morality (did you cross the legal line?) which lends itself to precise definitions (61). While under a legal system you have either transgressed a rule or not, within a shame morality the boundary is less clear: you are judged for the extent to which you have approximated an ideal, or fallen short with no clear demarcation of where you stand. Thus, an infectious sense of perpetual failing is at the center of the sanction of shame, not transgression *per se*. A guilt morality implies blame for having fallen short of a minimum threshold to which everyone is accountable, while shame adheres to a vague failure to attain an ideal that may be exceptional and singular, such as the failure to act heroically in the face of great danger. Guilt is defined by a morality of responsibilities and rights, of blame and fault with regard to the effect of one's conduct on others. Guilt lends itself to reprieve, considering social obligations, and the possibility of making reparations to others in order to restore a relationship that one has jeopardized through one's actions. As such, guilt does not question the fundamental validity of the actor in his relationships with others, only the validity of given actions. Shame, on the other hand, considers these relationships secondary to the more ambiguous question of one's overall validity. In this way, Morris tells us, one cannot find forgiveness for one's shame, and no act of compensation can restore a shamed subject, unless this action reveals some qualities of the self that more closely replicate the demands of an ideal.

Barring the option of forgiveness, the question remains: how does one find relief from shame? An escape from shame only occurs through a more radical transformation of the offending self, and of the relationship that self assumes toward the Other. And it is through this transformative force that shame derives a unique quality that I have referred to as shame's productivity: in seeking to abandon itself, the shamed subject invokes an inventiveness with regard to its relation to the Other that is entirely lacking in guilt's recuperative focus. As Morris puts it, "Shame leads to creativity; guilt to restoration" (62). From here Morris reaches a striking conclusion: "Shame connects with sight and guilt with hearing" (62). Shame involves the act of looking—of the self looking upon itself or the Other observing one's behavior from a distance and turning in disapproval. Shame is a wordless desire to disappear, to sink into the ground and hide ourselves from view, to exile ourselves from a community that cannot tolerate our existence. Guilt, on the other hand, invokes the "voice of conscience," as it formulates the words through which law is expressed, and strives to communicate terms for the restoration of one's status in the light of the correct measure of one's transgressions. "With guilt the urge is to communicate, to be listened to, to confess" (62).

In the first chapter of this book we explored the effects of the new racial sensibility in relation to the discursive field of woke literature, and those texts through which written and spoken words fix processes of white reracialization. It was argued that such forms of subjection, as the function of a dispositif, induce unsettling encounters with oneself, which generate waves of productivity and a certain novelty in relation to oneself and to the Other. In the second chapter we considered the dynamic of exposure in the shaping of that shame, where a panicked white subject undergoes his abandonment with a sense of dread and mystery, and with the consequence of a profound destabilization of the white subject, but also with a reactivation of the social field from which a shaming encounter emerges. And in this final chapter we will take up the problem of this shame and its transmutation into guilt as the shaming encounter is shaped around the problem of an interiority. In this chapter, an investigation of this transmutation of shame into guilt will be developed around two themes. First, through a reading of the curative mandate of the new racial sensibility as a therapeutic discourse, we find shame itself interpreted as a sickness, a puerile white dependency that must be rehabilitated into a mature sense of guilt. This transmutation, it is argued, inscribes a certain narrative and imposes a certain coherence: as a healing project, the abandonment and the atemporality of shame described in Chap. 3 is resolved into therapeutic project in which the white subject takes responsibility and feels guilt for an inner realm diagnosed as unhealthy. And in a second theme, this therapeutic assessment occurs as the shamed white subject is brought before the judgment of an omniscient Other, the object of certain white projections, inscribed with the authority to see into the white soul and prescribe a cure. This Other, and the powers of transmutation it expresses compose the functional core of the new racial sensibility, and today operate through a new network of regulative practices.

1 Privilege and the Road to Recovery

Within the conversations that drive the new racial sensibility, the word "privilege" operates in on oddly ambivalent sense, as that property of whiteness which stirs shame while at the same time capturing shame's drift in a web of guilt. Privilege is a juridical concept, one rooted in law and with a direct bearing on individual states of responsibility. Privilege implies a relation between one who is deprived of and one who unfairly derives a surplus. It imposes a zero-sum reduction which, by its very logic introduces a function of law and initiates a relation of guilt which imposes a certain obligation to remunerate, to pay back. Privilege is a "threshold," as Morris described: it is problem that implies the specific violation of a rule of fairness, the medium through which some quantity is subtracted from one side and added to another. But privilege is also a problem of scale: one can be a little or a lot privileged, and once the problem of privilege is posed it never goes away. To point this out is not to deny that privilege happens, nor that it should be redressed through such programs. Privilege, which participates in that function of power through which competing subjects take things from each other or give them back in guilt, remains a salient feature of white taken-for-grantedness, and as such the redress of privilege through law makes perfect sense. And yet, at the same time, the charge of privilege implies powerful effects of shame that are largely incompatible with the juridical framework of guilt itself. One does not exercise privilege the way one robs a bank or cheats on one's taxes. Privilege is ontological: it unfolds naturally from an interiority of which one is not entirely aware, from a condition which one is. To exercise privilege is a failure to meet the ideal of one who grasps oneself as equal to others. Privilege is not a simple choice, but reflects choices made in a state of unawareness, a sleep that derives from the inner state of one's whiteness

(Shotwell, 2011; Sullivan & Tuana, 2007; Bailey, 2007). In this way, privilege functions as a sort of pivot between shame and guilt, the point of their communication and in some ways their transmutation. We feel shame for being the kind of people that possess privilege, for our self-ignorance with regard to our privilege, yet we escape this shame, or we transmute this shame into guilt, as we accept our privilege as the expression of a deeper, interior state for which we are responsible, and as we make amends and pledge recompense for the harm that this inner condition has done to others. For this to work and for this transmutation to occur, we must invest the lens through which the Other detects this privilege, and through which the white subject is exposed in its shame and returned to itself in guilt. In this regard, privilege's inscrutability to oneself, and the capacity of the Other to sense and to name privilege, to draw out this privilege in a scene of exposure, serve a most significant function in enabling this transmutation to occur. Indeed, the portrayal of privilege's fugitive character no doubt serves the purpose of qualifying its call out as an indisputable accomplishment of juridical acumen. The Other, bearing the ability to detect and expose a privilege of which the white subject is largely unaware, must also be the Other capable of judging it, of prescribing its remediation and of transmuting a shameful condition into guilty actions (Rothenberg, 2004). The very detection of privilege demands, in a sense, a certain capacity for paranoid judgment. Shannon Sullivan, in her book *Revealing Whiteness: The Unconscious Habits of White Privilege*, has traced the ruse of white racism to a pattern of deception and duplicity rooted in a guileful habit distinguished for its cunning:

> It is no accident that it is difficult to hear the soft patter of white privilege. White privilege goes to great lengths not to be heard. Habits of white privilege are not merely nonconscious or preconscious. [There is] strong resistance to the conscious recognition of racism that characterizes habits of white privilege. As unconscious, habits of white privilege do not merely go unnoticed. They actively thwart the process of conscious reflection on them, which allows them to seem non-existent even as they continue to function. (Sullivan, 2006, pp. 5–6)

Privilege is the elusive folk-devil that has to be tracked and captured. Yet the multiple meanings implied by this term suspend the white subject somewhere between shame and guilt: as she becomes aware of her privilege, she is ashamed for the lecherous dependencies and the malformed character that privilege implies, just as the contemplation of the harm her privilege does to others draws her into the sphere of guilt. Privilege, as that attribute for which we can feel both shame and guilt, or shame evolving into guilt, gives shame a place to go, a story to tell and a task to complete, although with guilt, one must accept that this work will never be done, that the recompense demanded of a guilty act can never be fully paid, and that one must remain forever bound to the managerial task of a never-ending payment on a perpetual debt. Privilege, in this sense, serves as a pivot, a point of conversion where shame is apprehended, identified and transmuted into guilt. Privilege is the point of intersection between sickness and badness, the place where shame and guilt communicate with each other, or where a certain interior metamorphosis takes place. As such, privilege provides the scene for a durable and ongoing program. Robin DiAngelo is explicit in describing the problem of white privilege not as a moral issue, but as an environmental and cultural condition from which one should not imagine one can escape, arguing for the need to extract racism from the "good-bad binary" and to consider it instead as a point on an ever-receding horizon.

> Racism is so deeply woven into the fabric of our society that I do not see myself escaping from that continuum in my lifetime. ... Conceptualizing myself on an active continuum changes the question from whether I am or am not racist to a much more constructive question: Am I actively seeking to interrupt racism in this contest? And perhaps even more importantly, how do I know? (Di Angelo, 2018, p. 87)

DiAngelo is adamant that diversity training is a life-long commitment, and that to even suppose that it might end is itself evidence of the necessity for its redoubling and extension. The new racial sensibility's work, as the endless harvesting and bailing of shame (am I a racist?) as guilt (have I done enough to interrupt my racism?) has no terminal point precisely because it acts on a condition that the subject can never fully transcend: one can move along a continuum of scale, from more to less racist, but one can never cross a certain threshold beyond which guilt would end. The pull of racism's condition is something one can never escape. Conveniently for the apparatus, the subject of racism, as privileged, is always sick, always recovering, but never returned to health, its shame always pivoting into guilt, but never to the point of completion. One's rehabilitation is an ongoing and permanent feature of the primal failure of one's being. As such, we are always caught in the function of this apparatus, caught between shame and guilt: where whiteness sits perfectly suspended between the states of a condition and an action, something one is and something one does, the white subject finds a balance between an ontological shame and a moral guilt whose function lies in ensuring that the white subject will remain always in treatment. Whiteness, like the subject of sexual repression, is always emerging, never emerged, from its deplorable state. In this way, shame and guilt attain a certain functional equilibrium, where the work of overcoming our privilege through the efforts of a certain inner voyage operates as the perfect hinge, the point of a certain transfer between shame and guilt, but also between subject and subject-to.

Overcoming privilege implies a narrative of recovery not unlike that applied to such conditions as alcoholism, co-dependency, trauma, drug addition, over-eating or negative thoughts. Such narratives operate at a certain intersection of medicine and morality: one is afflicted by a condition, which one must confront with the conviction of a moral project in a gesture of responsibility. Recovery tells a story of one's evolution from illness to health, but also a developmental process in which the subject takes responsibility for her health, evolving from simple being to action and, in a sense, from shame to guilt. Morris' characterization helps to explain this trajectory, and how it is that shame has historically had such a bad reputation. As Morris suggests, the very condition of shame is subject to a certain stigma, regarded as an incomplete condition, the object of a certain program of improvement and rehabilitation. Shame has, for a long time, been reviled for its immaturity, particularly when contrasted with guilt. Shame is often cast as a self-involved emotion whose inward orientation renders the shamed subject fundamentally narcissistic, unable to assess its behaviors from the standpoint of others and thus unable to take public account for its actions. This quality is particularly apparent when contrasted with the responsible moral capacities associated with guilt. As Morris notes, guilt is rule bound, the attitude of a subject capable of empathic identification with an Other to whom she has done harm, and it is through this identification that she is therefore capable of perceiving her own actions from the Other's standpoint (Lewis, 1971b). Shame's immaturity stems from its inability to do this. The shamed subject grasps the Other only as an indistinct figure of over-identification and abandonment across a ruptured interocular relation. Such an Other leads the subject to focus less on the validity of her actions toward this Other than on the degraded quality of a self that is disclosed under the Other's withdrawn gaze. Shame's preoccupation with an aberrant self-discovery, it is believed, renders the shamed subject self-absorbed and infantile, a trope that plays on both historical and biographical registers.

According to Freud, shame is a reaction-formation that dams up prohibited libidinal drives in response to the threat of direct censure of the community. As such it is an outwardly oriented response to the fear of a public sanction, although this sanction is directed at impulses (aggressive, erotic) to which the subject herself may raise no particular objection, possessing as she does no internal mechanism of judgment or prohibition. In other words, in remaining focused on external censure, shame has not undergone a process of Oedipal development through which the repudiation of prohibited impulses would be carried on internally as a function of the subject's own conscience. It is for this reason that shame remains tied thematically to the scene of an exposure before a representative of the social order who sees through into the indecent reality of what the shamed subject secretly is. Indeed, for Freud, exposure of an unsightly body before a disapproving audience constitutes a central thread of the shame narrative. Freud describes a dream in which shame feelings are concentrated specifically on the moment of nakedness and exposure before others: "Suddenly you will become aware that you are in rags, naked and dusty. You will be seized with a nameless shame and dread, you will seek to find covering to hide yourself, and you will awake bathed in sweat" (Freud, 1955, p. 265). The uniquely outward facing character of shame anxiety is what defines it as an infantile version of reaction formations that will later be developed in the moral self-monitoring of the super-ego—a process of maturation through which feelings of shame are surpassed by feelings of guilt.

Adjacent to Freud's story of psychic development is another developmental narrative in which shame is reviled for its immaturity, this time playing out on the socio-historical register. In Ruth Benedict's portrayal, "shame cultures," are depicted as retrograde formations of traditional societies, practices of moral self-assessment that remain embedded in the judgments of closely integrated publics, expressed through dense networks of social obligation and formalized commitment. In contrast to shame cultures, more developmentally advanced "guilt cultures" allow autonomous moral self-reflection commensurate with higher levels of individuation, wherein solitary consideration takes the place of public sanction or adherence to protocol. If modernity differentiates the individual, guilt is the moral emotion into which shamed subjects ultimately mature, and it is only in a state of maturity that individuals are able to extend beyond an infantile preoccupation with social approval and to relate, responsibly, to others as the bearers of a fully formed moral self-awareness (Benedict, 2005, pp. 222–227). Tangney and Dearing summarize this predicament: "rather than promoting other-oriented empathic concern, the acute self-focus of shame is likely to foster self-oriented personal distress responses" (Tangney & Dearing, 2002, p. 83). As a consequence, shame, they argue, citing Martin Hoffman (2000, p. 56), reflects the indeterminate condition of an "egoistic drift," an unstable, undifferentiated relation to the Other which leaves the shamed ego ill-formed and infantile, unable to enact any sort of empathic relation, and thus to take responsibility for its own conduct. If moral maturity requires the negotiation of responsibilities through the adoption of the standpoint of the Other across well-marked interpersonal boundaries, egoistic drift, resulting from a split identification between the Other's assessment and the shamed subject's own self-regard, pries the subject loose from itself, dispersing it across the blurred intersubjective space of shamed self-awareness. Put differently, in shame, the subject that should be coherent enough to grasp the Other as Other, to see oneself clearly through the eyes of this Other and to make amends for bad actions taken toward this Other remains instead preoccupied with a panicked fantasy of what the Other has seen, and with what the Other has discovered oneself to be. In fantasy, the shamed subject is unmoored from itself as a consequence of the traumatic experience of a self-discovery brought on by its exposure before strangers. Development from shame to guilt is a process that begins to correct this situation through a tale of maturation and growth that is at once psychological, biographical, historical and moral, and the agent charged with relating this narrative is resolutely therapeutic.

In an oblique sort of way these characterizations of shame's moral immaturity resonate with images of whiteness that circulate through the new racial sensibility. Whiteness, in its privilege is a malady from which whites must recover. Whiteness, as immaturity, clings childishly to an exceptionalism through which the Other is reduced to a figment of racial projection, either an object of repudiation or a figure of fetishistic investment. The immature white subject as fragile, as savior or as consumed with white denial is in any case an infantile, narcissistic subject that cannot stand on its own and depends on an unacknowledged racial dividend, paid through the obliteration of the subjectivity of the Other, for the maintenance of its own identity. Immersed in infantile white fantasies, such a shamed subject lacks the soldierly commitments of the empathic white ally who has worked through these issues and has emerged with an empathic competence, a racial sixth sense. For this reason appeals to shame sit uneasily with the new racial sensibility's rhetoric of introspective therapeutic labor. Shame is what white people have to grow out of if they are to truly awaken from their racial slumber. Surely shame, therefore, is too immature, too narcissistic and too preoccupied with the trauma of its own exposure for the hard work of white self-interrogation. Even the proposal that the self-involvement of shame might constitute the basis for an anti-racist reconstruction of whiteness seems to conjure the worst aspects of a self-consumed whiteness that again, and by a more devious path, seeks to wash its hands of its responsibility for black suffering (Ahmed, 2004). Surely the work of anti-racism would be more capably conducted with a sense of responsibility that can be more fully attained in a wholly mature spirit of guilt.

Such was the consensus among many critics in their response to a proposal from the South African philosopher Samantha Vice, who in 2010 published an article titled "How Do I Live In This Strange Place" (Vice, 2010). Vice proposed that the challenges facing white South Africans in their pursuit of a morally good life in the post-Apartheid moment might be met through a stance of shamed silence and a wholesale withdrawal of whites from public discourse, so that they might attend to the necessary philosophical activity required for the reconstruction of white subjectivity itself—a seemingly innocuous suggestion not inconsistent with sentiments expressed in the new racial sensibility that whites refrain from "recentering whiteness" in conversations on race. But Vice's proposal was interpreted instead as a valorization of white self-involvement as such, and of a moral posture whose effect, it was alleged, was to exempt the white subject from those responsibilities that should rightly be responded to in guilt (328). Insincere shame further reifies white privilege, further valorizing the general habits of inwardness and withdrawal that already typify what some consider the narcissistic character of whiteness itself (333). For critics on the academic left, the reconstructive labor of white shame detached from the concrete work of moral responsibility could only amount to a flight into what Adrienne Rich termed "white solipsism" (Rich, 1979, p. 299). As one of Vice's harshest critics put it, "White souls can be saved and whiteness can be redeemed at the same time as most Black people continue to live in poverty" (Milazzo, 2017, p. 562). Indeed, the stigma of shame's immaturity extends beyond academic discourse, and is well embedded within the popular reception of the new racial sensibility.

Actress Rosanna Arquette discovered as much following a 2019 Twitter post in which she declared "I'm sorry I was born white and privileged. It disgusts me... And I feel so much shame." Pointing to her immense wealth and palatial residence, critics disparaged her declaration as a reflection of her privileged status, labeling her a "white-hating white woman" (Henderson, 2019). Such discussions are replete with those paranoid sensibilities, rightly or not, that characterize the new racial sensibility. Shame is a posture, a screen, a mask, behind which dwell enemies: racial infantilism and a lingering violence.

Yet, such rejections of white shame themselves serve a certain function that I think is worth examining. We have already seen how shame brings self-awareness and a sense of the opening of the self: shame traumatizes the white subject through a certain exposure, which unfolds a unique and uncanny white encounter. Shame, as a consequence of the abandonment it imposes, ignites a sporadic inventiveness that seeks alternative pathways through the racial field, extending to the Other in new ways. Yet, at the same time, through the new racial sensibility and the apparatus through which it operates, this unstable inventiveness is countered with the effect of a certain closing, as shameful self-exposure is translated into the language of an interior view for which we take responsibility, conferring a formal relation across which morally regrettable qualities might be assessed and accounted for, and harms redressed, conveying responsibility and guilt. Through the new racial sensibility and its narrative of recovery, appeals to guilt, not shame, are mobilized to subsume and constrain what the dispositif considers shame's "egoistic drift." White people are asked to get in touch with parts of themselves they had perhaps intentionally sealed off, and to make amends for the harmful effects of habitual actions that stem from this unresolved interiority. In other words, through a certain therapeutic mandate, shame is made to mature into guilt. This guilt expresses the emotional style required of a political program centered on the need to take responsibility for unearned privilege and for harm directly or indirectly inflicted on others (even as "white guilt" itself is so frequently disavowed as an indulgent alternative to concrete action and solidarity work) (Baldwin, 1985). Guilt, through the sense of accountability it imposes and through the reintegration it secures, compresses shame's egoistic drift into the responsible form signified by a responsible white subject, on the road to recovery from its states of privilege. Indeed, within the discourse of the new racial sensibility, the remaking of shame into guilt is the primary aim of a unique therapeutic rationale. To fully understand this process of the transmutation of shame into guilt, we must first delve more deeply into the broader racial logic that underpins therapeutic reason itself.

2 Therapeutic Alchemy

To speak of a therapeutic ethos is to draw together many strands of thought which variously combine a range of elements. At heart, a therapeutic ethos is a way of telling stories about change and transformation that derive significant support from the interiorizing motif of the psychological sciences and the medicalizing imperative upon which they are fashioned: one goes into therapy with the hopes of getting in touch with forces residing inside oneself, of curing, removing or diminishing an illness, discomfort or pathology that one senses within. Often these stories give form to the biographical narrative itself, confirming a sense of purpose and narrative identity. As such, the therapeutic ethos, as a medicalizing operation, relates a story of recovery through a series of successive stages. Through the therapeutic cure, time is subjected to a process of reordering around the aim of rehabilitation and restoration. One makes progress in therapy, one has therapeutic breakthroughs, one moves along a certain path as one seeks to put to rest anxieties, phobias and recurrent emotional patterns that have troubled one since childhood. The inward journey is an incremental one. Sometimes this story takes the form of a curative quest, a long struggle to overcome a deforming malady, while at other times it is aligned with a bio-somatic teleology, the developmental path of a growth toward the realization of one's inner truth, the production of new capacities or the actualization of the self, such as we saw in the first chapter with the staged theory of white anti-racist identity. In any case, this story is replete with moral connotations in which earned wellness is equated with moral maturity and the attainment of virtue. To remain sick is itself a small sin. Sickness, as Talcott Parsons famously argued, provides a "sick role" which imposes obligations and responsibilities on the patient and on others, and in this way shares many structural similarities with social categories more commonly understood through a moral lens (Parsons, 1951, p. 285). It is everyone's responsibility to admit to their illness and cooperate with treatment, to get help or to "get their shit together" by undertaking the appropriate form of therapeutic work. Indeed, as is often argued by critics of societal medicalization, the expanding jurisdiction of medical authority has enabled a shift from "badness to sickness," as medical criteria come to displace traditional standards of morality, although there is a sense in which this shift is never complete, as sickness today nevertheless brings with it newer and more urgent moral obligations (Conrad & Schneider, 1992). Through this process, sick being is evolved into moral doing as shame matures into guilt. A bumpersticker distributed by Religious Society of Friends, a Quaker organization in Albany, New York, perfectly crystallizes this framing of racism as a condition that sits ambiguously between the blurred threshold of the moral and the medical: "Racism: Our National Disease: Getting Sick Was Not Our Fault, Getting Well Is Our Responsibility." Wellness, in this respect, involves a resolute coming to terms with oneself through a sort of inward journey, and as such implies the correction of those pathological preoccupations that hold back one's healthy, moral development. The road to the therapeutic cure of white racism runs through a condition of healthy guilt, which requires us to mature out of the infantile state of a formless, egoistic shame.

The trajectory of such development imposes its own sense of time. It provides a future and a goal, outlining a path that gives us back the time that shame took away. Where shame's time was stalled through abandonment, guilt's time, through the lens of a therapeutic narrative, begins to flow again. Guilt's time connects us with others as we learn to dig back into repressed memories and project our progress in our growth from immaturity toward our expected moral cure. One looks forward to a future in which, as Foucault notoriously stated about sex, race will be good again, although we must be patient and humble as we undertake this difficult work. With such a future in mind, time seems to emerge from the frozen, traumatic state to which shame had abandoned it. Therapeutic time is time shared with a certain Other, between the sick, but recovering, therapeutic subject and the therapeutic authority that ministers over her recovery. In this way, therapeutic time is a social time, a time of shared progress—or so it seems. But it is also a time heavily scripted by the conventions that surround it. It is a time that only moves along a single path and only goes in one direction, while leaving relative positions intact. In this sense, it is a social time, but a social time conceived without the plastic quality, or the dynamism of social life itself. The conversion or transmutation of shame into guilt provides a certain programmatic frame: it is the work of a therapeutic narrative—a process with an aim and a purpose that attains a specific valence as it is applied to the problem of white shame. Once I was troubled and didn't understand why, so I set about studying my inner life until I came to a new understanding, all under the guidance of one who knew better than I. And in this way I was cured. This is a great story that undoes the trauma of abandonment, though it is also rather unsurprising and dull, easily predicted and channeled into manageable forms. And like every great story, it requires a competent story teller, a raconteur capable of relating this narrative in a convincing way.

The work of one such narrator can be described: Resmaa Menakem is an author, commentator and psychotherapist specializing in trauma and somatic therapy as they relate to the effects of racism. Identifying as a "therapist, healer & author," his role as a counselor has seen him serve at a variety of centers based in his home city of Minneapolis, offering counseling services to youth, women and members of underserved communities struggling with issues of domestic violence, racism and poverty. His resumé describes a rising star on the American racial scene, author of several *New York Times* best-selling books, visits to the Oprah Winfrey and Dr. Phil shows, as well as appearances on popular podcasts and radio programs. He is the founder of the Cultural Somatics Institute, which defines its commitment to "somatic abolitionism," understood as "an embodied way of living that builds resilience and discernment, upends white-body supremacy, and trains our bodies, individually and collectively, to rediscover their natural alignment" (Cultural Somatics Training Institute, 2022). That Menakem's work contributes to the societal process of overcoming racial inequality is not in question, and there are many arguments that could be raised regarding its value in working through, on both a personal and societal level, many of the dispositions that shape white supremacist attitudes. Alongside that assessment, however, another thread of inquiry points out the more subtle influences of Menakem's approach, which are layered in their meanings and multiple in their effects.

Menakem's unique contribution is with linking racial trauma to bodily experiences, and the prescription of a set of techniques involving breathing, mindfulness and meditative exercises around the wider project of dispelling the residue of "white body supremacy," an internalized set of trauma-based attitudes and habits that shape our bodily sensibilities. This trauma is detected not only in black and white bodies, but also blue bodies—in the bodily sensibilities of law enforcement officers who are the most direct agents of racist violence. In 2017, Menakem published *My Grandmother's Hands: Racialized Trauma and the Pathway to Mending Our Hearts and Bodies*, a guide to the healing of white-body supremacy through exercises and commentary derived from neuroscience and somatic healing techniques (Menakem, 2017). The title refers to the hands of his grandmother, a sharecropper whose stunted fingers bore the trauma of labor in cotton fields she was forced to undergo from a very young age. In a chapter titled "Mending the White Heart and Body," the author provides a set of exercises white people might undertake to interrogate and overcome their conditions of white-body supremacy. These include reflecting on their own feelings of anxiety when in the presence of black people, allowing black people to take their place in lines for various services or leaving larger tips for black waiting staff. The aim of these actions is not only to confront and reverse patterns of social inequality for which one bears a specific responsibility, but to "heal" oneself, where healing is blended with other processes of maturation, growth and therapeutic recovery from a state of traumatic self-absorption. Menakem puts it this way:

> We all need to grow up if we are to live full, meaningful lives. A pernicious side effect of white-body supremacy is that it allows (and sometimes encourages) white Americans to choose not to grow up. They can stay purposely blind to their own white-body supremacy and trauma; repeatedly deny or refuse to address it... For generations, white-body supremacy allowed many white Americans to avoid developing the full range of necessary skills for navigating adulthood. Instead of building resilience, and accepting the full pain and grief and disappointment of human existence, they outsourced some of that pain, grief, and disappointment to dark-skinned bodies. ... Paradoxically, these efforts made many white Americans more vulnerable to trauma and caused them to feel more fragile and threatened, in the same way that overprotecting a child encourages him or her to become a helpless, frightened adult. This is the ultimate irony of white-body supremacy: in the name of protecting and serving white Americans, it has done immense harm to them. (Menakem, 2017, p. 113)

In this passage, the "outsourcing" of pain is the mark of a certain traumatic narcissism, a self-absorbed failure to convey recognition to the Other. The harm that this narcissism brings, in this regard, is the illness—somatic trauma—that Menakem's method seeks to cure, although the illness itself shares resonances equally with both medical and moral criteria, both sickness and badness, and the path out from this illness is one that blends with trajectories of growth rooted in stories of moral maturity. In other words, Menakem is curing these white people by helping them to mature out of their illnesses. This requires them to become people who can see themselves and their actions through the eyes of others—people who no longer outsource their suffering but recognize the Other as she is, who see and assume responsibility for the harm done to Others, and who experience mature guilt in place of infantile shame.

Menakem's is a demand that grounds the charge of guilt, not just in our bad choices, but in an inner state of an abnormal being, a hidden trauma of which we are not completely aware though which may be resolved if we venture into some interior theater of engagement. Such a resolution would induce a complex admixture of shame and guilt, or shame that is in the same moment transmuted into guilt. The shameful state of our unaware existence, it is argued, can be overcome as we engage our interior conditions, wake up to ourselves, take responsibility for our actions and undertake a set of programs necessary to mitigate the harmful effects that our whiteness has imposed on others. Again, guilt itself is not celebrated within those literatures that compose the discourse of the new racial sensibility as an adequate response to the challenges of white anti-racism, although, even in its renunciation, the inevitability of a certain guilt feeling is logically implied. Robin DiAngelo writes:

> I don't see my efforts to uncover how race shapes my life as a matter of guilt. I know that because I was socialized as white in a racism-based society, I have a racist worldview, deep racial bias, racist patterns, and investments in the racist system that has elevated me. Still, I don't feel guilty about racism… but I am responsible for my role in it. To the degree that I have done my best in each moment to interrupt my participation, I can rest with a clearer conscience. (149)

In these sentences, guilt is not disavowed per se, but is relegated to a certain level of secondary importance in relation to one's more pragmatic responsibilities. Yet guilt is also acknowledged as an unavoidable consequence of one's emergence from the white condition. It is an affect indispensable to white moral conduct and therapeutic growth, but also a feeling one must not dwell on too long and that must be immediately converted into "interrupting" actions allowing one to derive a "clearer conscience." Which suggests that the problem of guilt is more tolerated than renounced, and continues to dog the subject even into this rehabilitated state. It is my suggestion that this tolerance for guilt serves the purpose of a certain transmutation. Guilt accomplishes the larger function of managing and containing, even suppressing through concealment, the underlying and deeply disruptive effect of shame.

Through the effect of the healing narrative in which shame is matured into guilt, a certain form is stamped onto shame's unstable drift, covering over the frightful self-encounter that shame opens up with the image of a stable inner life, on a clear course to improvement. Guilt holds the white racial subject in place through the inscription of a certain racial obligation, an interior debt that serves as a fixed point, an unchanging element within the white subject. In shame we seek to abandon ourselves, to escape ourselves, to make ourselves new and to extend to the Other across a new social field yet to be imagined, if only through trauma. Through the lens of guilt, however, this sense of possibility is suppressed. The subject that committed a past offense, and the subject that must make amends and pay compensations, has been "caught," and must remain coherent over the course of time. "Owning one's whiteness" usually implies such a temporal consistency, reducing oneself back to a past one had previously denied, pinning one's present and future to some primordial act originating from the dark well of an interior condition. Efforts to break that continuity are themselves further evidence of one's condition of guilt. Where the shamed subject found himself trapped in time, prompting a sporadic if compulsive inventiveness, the subject of guilt sets that time in alignment with a therapeutic convention, finding a certain stride in the shared work of therapeutic recovery. Time flows again, but only in one direction, from a fixed subject to an equally fixed Other, who mediates and directs that subject's recovery. The direction of this time is incremental, clearly cut and well-rehearsed. This is, after all, the continuity across time that characterizes not just the therapeutic but the juridical subject, who takes responsibility in the present for actions taken in the past, and pledges to repair the effect of those actions in the future.

Guilt, in this regard, has a specific use for the sense of interiority that characterizes the therapeutic ethos. Guilt, like illness, is a debt relation: it is a promise to pay to the Other what is owed and to make good on a certain balance—a commitment which requires a clear economy of ill deeds and ill effects, of crimes committed, wounds suffered, and balances due, bad interests and bad intentions, anchored in a great interior life. After all, what better place from which to pay one's debts than a place so personal and forbidden as to make the very act of payment itself seem like a kind of suffering, a labored, confessional disclosure emanating from a place the very inaccessibility of which validates payment as real and legitimate. But for such payment to seem valid what is also required is a stable Other capable of mediating responsibility through a stable set of demands and a coherent narrative of remuneration. Guilt requires a steady gaze before which it can expose itself and a hidden realm from which secrets can be revealed, painfully. Guilt requires a steady gaze before which it can expose itself and a hidden realm from which secrets can be revealed, painfully. By so doing, the guilty white subject measures itself and gauges its progress before a gaze that can be precisely replicated within—an unbroken gaze that does not, as in the ocular relation of the shaming scene, withdraw itself or look away. What is required is the fixed stare of the stern judge. In this way, guilt requires an Other who, if it does not exist, must be invented, in the white mind, as an Other capable of penetrating white interiority, of seeing into oneself, imposing consistent judgments and assessing one's debts. An Other capable of telling such a story is one invested with the power of pronouncing on the hidden world of one's white soul. It is an Other capable of assessing one's innocence or guilt, of remembering one's past and anticipating one's future, of narrating one's recovery from a corrupted, criminal state, of adjudicating one's failures and prescribing a moral debt, even as that adjudication is indefinitely postponed, extending the work of the guilty subject in an ongoing exercise against an ever-receding horizon. In other words, this is an Other very close to the Other of the exposing shameful gaze, replete with its paranoid sensibilities, although, importantly, key modifications have crept in: this is the gaze of a therapeutic expert whose regard is not broken and who does not turn away but remains fixed and clear, who sees and admonishes every detail, whose presence is demarcated and whose demands are imposed programmatically. And it is before the gaze of this Other that shame undergoes its alchemical transmutation, emerging as a preponderant sense of guilt.

3 Otherness and the Privatization of Shame

Psychoanalytic treatments of racism have made great use of the function of projection. In this psychic operation, Melanie Klein discovered a set of processes by which those internalized emotional states we cannot tolerate in ourselves are externalized through an act of projective identification onto others, who stand in for those elements of ourselves that we do not wish to acknowledge (Klein, 1946). Projective identification can be distinguished from simple projection by the intensity of its enactment and by the measure of its impact on the Other. While it may be commonplace to disown things we don't like about ourselves, our nervousness or greed, by complaining that our friends or neighbors are in fact nervous or greedy, projective identification goes further by actually requiring that the Other assumes these disavowed qualities, and that the function of projection is only complete when others have been induced to actually become nervous or greedy themselves. Through the process of the reracialization of whiteness, the white subject enacts a form of projection, though, as I mentioned earlier, it is not the socially prohibited functions of the id that are transposed onto a degraded Other but precisely those cerebral, moral operations of the super-ego which are inscribed on the Other's powers of judgment and insight. In this way, the reracialization of whiteness induces the inverse effect of classical, white "dominative" racialization: the white subject is degraded while the Other is elevated to the status of an all-seeing judge, capable of establishing law and assessing guilt. However, as I have tried to argue, through such an inversion, white reracialization also serves the effect of replicating the very sequence and the very order, albeit in a gentler form, of the original racism it ostensibly seeks to undo. This is what I mean when I claim that the new racial sensibility preserves rather than transforms the racism it seeks to abolish.

As such, guilt, or the threat of guilt, is an emotion that brings certain comforts that are analogous with the comforts of racism. Guilt confirms our boundaries and tells us when we are and are not in accord with the moral expectations of our neighbors. While we suffer from guilt feelings, the felt possibility of guilt confers coherence on a self that stands before the law. As Emile Durkheim argues, the possibility of guilt is what saves us from anomic anxiety. Where there appears no figure adequate to the task of judging us for our guilt, we experience listlessness and ontological insecurity, and we tend to seek out such figures, producing them often through our fantasies and investments. In the medical realm, projection of the power to judge (and hence to cure) is central to therapeutic authority. Through projection, we convert teachers, doctors or fitness coaches into guilt-bestowing authorities, or we invent new authorities through acts of ideation. Freud notes the case in which the therapist himself is selected for this purpose by a patient who refuses to get better in treatment, but instead only gets worse: "[this is a] sense of guilt, which is finding its satisfaction in the illness and refuses to give up the punishment of suffering" (Freud, 1960, p. 50).

It is not a great leap to conclude a similar operation occurring within the illness of white racism, and through the function of judgment the white subject projects onto the Others who oversee his recovery from such a disabling condition. And, as we have seen, it is the function of the dispositif of white racialization to induce such projections through an operation in which shame is reexperienced as guilt. Such a transmutation does not imply simple elimination. Reexperiencing shame as guilt does not banish shame, but, I would argue, conceals it, withdrawing it from the fragmented and interrupted relation to the Other from which its trauma was induced and through which its creativity was expressed. Guilt doesn't resolve shame, evolve it, replace it or diminish it. Guilt technicizes shame, withdrawing it from the dynamic field through which it interacts with the Other into a private realm where it simmers noxiously. Guilt stifles shame's ambivalent expressions, veiling the blushes through which shame calls out to the Other and carves out new pathways across frozen social scenes. Guilt privatizes shame, withdrawing it into an interior space and into a fixed relation with a therapeutic Other, wherein it is suppressed as a social force and exorcised from the public realm, forcing it into hiding.

In her influential psychoanalytic treatments of shame, Helen Lewis has argued that in contemporary social life intolerable shame is ubiquitous but frequently concealed or "bypassed," banished from conscious awareness and from shared mediation while at the same time being allowed to swirl around us in myriad hidden and disguised forms (Lewis, 1971b; Scheff & Retzinger, 2001, p. 13). As Lewis observed in a series of psychotherapeutic studies, subjects possess an array of mechanisms through which overt or undifferentiated shame can be readily converted into bypassed or hidden shame: what is initially experienced as an intense surge, a "wince, blow or jolt," is, Lewis argues, within seconds subjected to a distancing effect through which the shamed subject engages in rapid intellectual, cognitive or verbal behavior (Lewis, 1971b, p. 197). The nervous and often flailing chatter that her patients exhibit reflects the preoccupation of the shamed subject with a form of talk through which shame feelings can be avoided as they are reexperienced as guilt. Under the guise of speech, particularly guilty speech, shame is coerced into the syntactic form of that which can be communicated and negotiated with the Other, explained, compensated, regretted and forgiven. Lewis recounts stories in which her psychoanalytic patients, beset with feelings of shame, make quick recourse to verbal explanation, rapid and manic justifications and other means of transposing shame feelings into a negotiable relation with the therapist. "A sequence from by-passed shame affect, could be traced into 'distancing' or self-imaging, in which the … patient became involved in thinking about what he would think if he were the therapist thinking about the patient." In other words, the bypassing of shame is attained through an act of identification with an Other who thinks about the subject, effectively assuming the function of the super-ego (423). This movement implies a recasting of the role of the condemning Other from the one who glances and looks away, thereby triggering feelings of shame, to one who sustains a fixed and ongoing judgmental gaze, for it is in response to this engaging look that it becomes possible to identify with the Other, to adopt the Other's view of oneself and hence to explain oneself.

> This defense, which is best described as "by-passing" shame feeling, does not obliterate the recognition of shame events, but appears to prevent the development of shame feelings. This by-passing of shame is accomplished by a 'distancing' maneuver. The self views itself from the standpoint of the 'other,' but without much affect. The person wonders what he would think of himself if he were in the position of the 'other.' The content of the ideation in question concerns shame events, but without shame affects. (Lewis, 1971a, p. 428)

Such an operation, Lewis argues, does not fully extinguish shame feelings, but allows them to hide, establishing sufficient distance from these feelings for them to remain beneath the threshold of immediate awareness. Hiding in this sense implies the muting of shame's communicative function, but also the stifling of the reflective character through which shame views the self subjectively, through fresh eyes. This implies a reclothing of shame in the garb of guilt. Thus clothed, shame hides, though it also intensifies its effect, spreading and infiltrating through all the pores of personal and public life.

Bypassing through a transmutation to guilt is not the only means by which shame goes into hiding. Another possibility comes with the transmutation of shame, into anger, rage and violence. Taking up Lewis' analysis, Scheff and Retzinger have described a set of emotional sequences by which intolerable shame is transmuted into aggression that can be directed not just against the self, as in guilt, but against the Other presumed to be responsible for such shame in the form of resentment and hostility. What they term shame-anger spirals, in which an accelerating and intensifying feedback loop between shame and rage traps the subject in a pattern of seemingly unstoppable violence, is observed in patterns of male violence, hyper-nationalistic aggression and other responses to perceived humiliation.

Such spirals no doubt explain a very different, though in some ways related white response to crises and shifts within the American racial order (Scheff, 1987, 1994; Scheff & Retzinger, 2001). The angry complaints of white nationalists of their "oppression" by feminists, racial justice activists and the multicultural state voice a response to what they perceive as the shaming exposure of whiteness before the gaze of an emerging black public who seek to "replace" them, and to which they respond with a pantomime military mobilization, complete with tiki-torches and home-made shields. But this explosive bypassing of shame is something quite different from the therapeutic treatment of white racial shame with which we are presently concerned, which relies on the more subtle methods of refined technique (Scheff, 1994).

In the case of guilt, through an empathic recovery of the viewpoint of the racial Other and the inscription of the Other with a certain authority to know and therefore to judge what becomes our "inner" psychic turmoil, the Other becomes, as Lewis argues, a point from which self-distancing and self-monitoring become possible. Lewis writes: "Shame affect is by-passed and replaced by watching the self from a variety of viewpoints" (Lewis, 1971a, p. 428). The distancing effects of this operation are, as Morris has shown us, juridical and legal, although, as I have already argued, they also represent an odd combination of the cognitive, the discursive and even the erotic.

> The unconscious gratification of being in a morally elevated state also sometimes keeps the state active beyond the time of expiation. 'He who despises himself,' wrote Nietzsche, 'thereby esteems himself as the despiser... When we train our conscience, it kisses as it bites.' The self, then may be caught in its own unconscious pride in being guilty, thus prolonging guilt rather than discharging it. The unconsciously perpetuated guilt takes the form of obsessive ideation. The self cannot stop its ideational activity. (432)

That such an erotics of guilt might be named as an intractable feature of the new racial sensibility does not draw into question guilt's importance within a broader political project. Certainly eroticism is everywhere in one form or another so it is natural that it might also be here, though what we learn from this particular eroticism is the wider function that guilt comes to serve as the agencies of guilty judgment are so invested with fantastic qualities. Moreover, the erotic investment spreads from the authorizing figure of judgment to the very textured nature of the Others' epistemic authority. The Other's knowledge, the very condition of being woke that we discussed in the introduction to this volume, opens up a world of forces and effects which the Other is presumed to know, worlds of authenticity and intensity that the white subject can only participate in through a fantastic identification with this Other. Where the subaltern brings a therapeutic cure, the white subject is roused from her racial slumber to greet this supercharged, hyperreal world in which the Other is thought to live with new eyes. In Ta-Nehisi Coates' memoire, *Between the World and Me*, whiteness is depicted as precisely the opposite of black knowing, as a state of self-willed unreality, as a Dream: "it is perfect houses with nice lawns," Coates writes: "It is Memorial Day cookouts, block associations, and driveways. The Dream is treehouses and the Cub Scouts. The Dream smells like peppermint but tastes like strawberry shortcake" (Coates, 2015, p. 11). That he can describe this Dream is only due to his exclusion from it, though this is an exclusion which, he tells his son, affords him an insight he would not readily trade. Black objectivity and the truth it accesses is a state that "brings you closer to the meaning of life, just as for others the quest to believe oneself white divides them from it."

> And I would not have you live like them. You have been cast into a race in which the wind is always at your face and the hounds are always at your heels. And to varying degrees this is true of all life. The difference is that you do not have the privilege of living in ignorance of this essential fact. (107)

For white readers of this passage, it would seem that black people possess not just the truth of the real world in all its seductive textures, but also the truth of white subjectivity itself—a truth from which white people are themselves painfully excluded, access to which can only be gleaned through the Other. It could plausibly be argued that faith in this truth is, in some ways, strategically necessary in the struggle against white supremacy, or that this faith constitutes the debt owed for long years of tyranny and exploitation. Yet, for the purpose of a reconstruction of whiteness from within, the fantasy of black omniscience, and of a blackness that possesses a special relationship to "the meaning of life" is a distracting, even a dangerous notion, opening onto, as it does, not just to a transmutation of shame but a covert erotics of guilt that only emerges through the judgment of one thought to possess a special access to reality. David Brooks, the white opinion writer for the *New York Times*, hailed Coates' book as a "great and searing contribution to public education... a slap and a revelation," an awakening of the senses that brings a certain obligation "to make sure the testimony is respected and sinks in.... you've filled my ears unforgettably" (Brooks, 2015).

In sum, the institutionalization of the gaze which makes it possible to reexperience shame as guilt, comes to serve, through the function of a certain projection, as a means of relieving shame feelings brought on by the reracialization of whiteness, of capturing and suppressing its movements and containing its possibilities, through a unique operation of bypassing. As guilt, these feelings are made to confess their truths, to fit within a formal economy of debts and obligations, of transparency before an all-seeing Other and to engage in an incremental process of recovery. Thus privatized, shame is hidden, withdrawn from the social field and from the Other's and one's own awareness, converted into a private pleasure and stripped of those dynamic qualities through which shame embeds us in our relations with others. Shame is muted, incorporated into a formal economy of debts and obligations while the social field is calcified and the subject pinned to itself.

One further point must be made with regard to this Other and it functions, and the ways in which this Other is conjured in the white imagination and through the discourses of the new racial sensibility. My claim is that the white subject's projection of a certain moral alterity onto the figure of this juridical and therapeutic Other is one that reproduces certain structures of racial Othering that have long operated at the heart of white racism. It is in this way, and by a sort of indirect process, that the new racial sensibility shares key features with that set of attitudes and investments that can be broadly grouped under the relation of racism itself. As the figure of a white conscience, the racial Other has long been made to serve as a screen for the images of white psychic projection, and thus to do the work of the maintenance of an unstable white ego. In more classical formations of white racism, the Other becomes the stand-in for those qualities that white subjects distain most about themselves, qualities of scatological desire, sexual aggression, violence or impulsiveness which, according to a certain view, can be attributed to the id (Kovel, 1984). This time, however, the body, and the voice (and indeed, the eyes) of the Other are appropriated as screens for a very different set of white projections: through the Other's gaze those functions of conscience associated, not with the id but with the super ego are at once externalized and experienced by a subject who savors the relief brought by certain feelings of guilt. The Other, through a function of projection, is made into an arbitrator who can see into the white subject's inner sanctum, an adjudicator of the subject's ongoing moral and psychic recovery, who can locate that guilt in the space of a certain therapeutic interiority, and in so doing reorder fragmented and unstable time around the narrative of a maturity from shame into guilt. Through this Other, the white subject can see into its own white being, though instead of abandoning itself in shame, it disciplines its egoistic drift into a debt relation from which it prescribes its recompense. It is an Other who cures and who heals, but also judges, and who in so doing remakes traumatic and generative shame into measured guilt.

To call this act of projection racist is perhaps to stretch the meanings of an already rhetorically exhausted word, and if it is racist, it is perhaps only so through a precise reversal of racism that is justified by a greater debt, a payment toward a necessary overcoming of racism itself. But if racist is too strong a word, then I think managerial will suffice, if by managerial we mean the management, and ultimately the reproduction of certain key elements of white racial subjectivity—and by extension, of the racial order from which this subjectivity derives. By this token, I would contend that to oppose the projections of this Other, as the final juridical, omniscient and therapeutic authority on matters of whiteness, is to oppose the racial order itself.

4 Subaltern Governmentality?

Beginning in 2019, two racial justice activists, Saira Rao and Regina Jackson, both women of color, began a program called Race2dinner. Race2dinner (2021) program consisted of a series of planned dinner parties where wealthy white women might meet to discuss the problem of racism, and specifically the topic of their complicity with racial inequality. These events developed from a series of conversations around Rao's 2018 bid for a congressional seat in Colorado in which she found herself repeatedly asked to engage her donors and supporters on the question of race. These one-on-one conversations grew tiring, Rao reports, prompting her to hold larger dinner events, hosted by participant attendees who, for fees upward of $5,000, could invite their friends for what promised to be intense and demanding conversations. Joined by Jackson, the events grew in number. Following the surge of interest in the politics of race in the summer of 2020, Race2dinner was holding, via zoom, several dinners a week. A website promoting the dinners lays the challenge squarely at the feet of the white women interested in hosting the events: "White women: let's talk about your racism and your complicity," "white women you need to sit in your discomfort." One activity included in the dinner involves going around the table and asking each participant "what was a racist thing you did recently," a tactic that reflects the belief shared by the organizers on the inevitability of emotional strain in the overcoming of white racism: "There is no growth without change" Writes Jackson, "and there is no change without pain. It's gonna be painful" (Door, 2020; Wida, 2020). The dinners prohibit crying and instruct participants not to derail the discussion with dissenting views or the disputation of key assumptions: "white women attending these dinners need to be committed to resisting white defenses and the host is prepared to interrupt white fragility so as not to derail the conversation" (race2dinner.com). Jackson describes this work: "This internal work is the hard work; it's the work that never ends," "Until you deal with your inner stuff—until you can say, 'I'm coming from a place where I recognize that I have these thoughts, and I'm working on it'—everything else is performing" (Fischer, 2021).

What is striking in this scene is not the will-to-govern revealed by the dinner's organizers. Their life experiences have no doubt shaped within them a deep seated desire to command such an audience in order to transform the conditions under which they have suffered, and in so doing to orchestrate some response to the forces of white racism that have shaped their lives. This all seems unsurprising and reasonable. What is striking is the investment of the dinner attendees themselves, and the will-to-*be*-governed that is expressed in their consent to, even their investment in these discussions. These women link the authority of the Other to impose discomfort with the derivation of a new self-transparency that such government promises. The place they imagine the event's organizers to occupy is one that binds their authority to judge with the capacity to see into and to open up a new therapeutic space, one that brings both shame and guilt, or a guilt that at the same time induces and conceals shame. This is an authority that is unique to our age, born of a democratic conviction to know, recognize and understand others across the divide of social inequality, and a profound belief in the integrity of psychological practice and the promise of psychic healing. It is an authority that responds to the need to find the resources within oneself necessary for the conferring of dignity where history and habit have conspired to deny it, and it is an authority principally conceived through the lens of a therapeutic enterprise. As such, this is an authority that unfolds a certain field of relations, a technology of the subject through which adjustments are made and rationalities are inscribed—a governmentality enacted through the figure of the subaltern itself.

"Can the Subaltern Speak?": when Gayatri Spivak posed this question in her landmark essay in 1988, subaltern, a term derived from a critical reading of Antonio Gramci's prison notebooks, signaled a population of marginal beings who, shut out from the privileges of citizenship, struggled to find voice and to describe their experiences in a public discourse organized around those conventions of representation and subjection from which they were excluded (Spivak, 1988). The text, considered foundational in such fields as subaltern studies and post-colonial theory, describes this silencing in structural terms: the subaltern was denied the capacity to speak through an exclusion that extended to the most basic assumptions through which Western self-understanding is fostered. The subaltern was more often spoken for, precisely by those intellectuals and political vanguards who assessed what the subaltern had to say in advance through the lens of their own ideological frameworks. Were the same question posed today, any answer given would have to take into account the startling success of critical discourses such as those pioneered by Spivak and others in reshaping much of what we take today to be our public morality, and in the reform of those codes through which speakers are qualified. This is not to deny that there continue to exist huge populations marginalized from public discourse through the representational biases around which such conversations are organized. Nor is it to deny that codes of public speech remain inordinately biased in terms of the populations whose speech they enable, and that calls for their reform are justified. Yet, representationally at least, the terms of this marginalization have shifted owing to the vastly developed powers of absorption and incorporation, of cooptation and mimicry (a set of media effects that were for a long time described as postmodern) which public discourse wields today. We have already seen how paranoia, as a means of survival practiced by the racially marginalized, is appropriated and transposed onto a means of therapeutic self-reflection practiced by well-meaning whites. Similarly, while global subaltern populations continue to struggle to speak, it is undeniable that a certain reified version, or a simulacrum of the subaltern gaze has since undergone a dramatic ascent, often emulated in corporate and governmental communications, emerging as an important point of reference in many discussions relevant to public life and personal conduct. Indeed, the subaltern position (which might say nothing of actual subalterns themselves), operates in many fields as that matrix through which certain judgments pass, certain transmutations are managed and certain pedagogical regimes are communicated. The subaltern position today provides an important nodal point through which governmental functions are carried out, and in particular, through which white interiority is deployed, produced, stabilized and captured in law and made subject to the normativity of a broader racial order. If the subaltern remains excluded from the representational order that would enable speech, the image of this subaltern, and the powers of juridical authority assigned to its image, are an unavoidable presence in public and organizational spaces today, even in the daily conducts of professional practice and in social life itself.

Mundane examples of the ubiquity of this new, governmental subaltern are easy to find: in the summer of 2021 the San Francisco International Airport opened its long awaited Harvey Milk terminal, named for the first openly gay American politician to attain national visibility before his murder in the 1970s. In 2019, the Massachusetts legislature approved a proposal to require all Boston busses to display the image of Rosa Parks in honor of the civil rights leader's heroic work. And in May of 2021, controversy flared over a recruitment video posted by a Federal agency to social media. In it, a Latinx woman strides the halls of a regal government building, relating in strong terms the challenges she had to overcome in securing her position at this organization.

> I am a woman of color. I am a mom. I am a cisgender millennial who has been diagnosed with generalized anxiety disorder. I used to struggle with imposter syndrome but at 36 I refuse to internalize misguided patriarchal ideas of what a woman can or should be. I am tired of feeling like I'm supposed to apologize for the space I occupy rather than intoxicate people with my effort, my brilliance. (CIA, 2021)

While conservatives complained about the willingness of public agencies to employ woke rhetoric to endear themselves to young workers and of the kind of face such a gesture presents to "our enemies," some on the left seized on this as proof of the politically regressive character of the new politics of identity, and its easy cooptation into the very halls of American empire itself. However one reads the significance of this video, that it was conceived as a recruitment tool for the CIA suggests that any effort to take up the question of the contemporary status of the subaltern must take into account the broader cooptation of this figure and of the view from below that she is purported to possess, as well as the ways in which the figure of the subaltern has been put to work in the service of new functions of government.

The subaltern's power to judge implies an equally authoritative power to know, and the institutional codification of subaltern judgment is reflected in the underlying patterns through which this knowledge is understood. In the previous chapter we considered the epistemic character of what I termed a paranoid racial view, one that possesses an overriding preoccupation with the veracity of the personal standpoint. Standpoint theory, or standpoint epistemology, understands the production of knowledge as reflective of the socially positioned, practical lifeworld experiences of the knower herself (Hartsock, 2004). To know is inevitably to know from somewhere, from the place where one sits, and it is from within those relations of power and oppression that the knower derives insight and awareness of the phantoms that haunt the life of power itself. Situated knowledge, in contrast to the unsituated objectivity from which universal knowing issues, is disreputable and corrupt, reducible to the material conditions from which it emerges rather than the timeless laws from which it claims to derive its authority. The situated knowing of the subaltern is a relation that exposes the malice, the brute domination that operates behind any pretense to universality. As such, perspectival knowing is unique and nonreproducible: it derives its validity from the particularity of its production, from memories of the violences it has endured, and for this reason it presumes that any reluctance to cooperate with its agenda could only be an extension of that violence itself. An item that has circulated across many anti-racist websites is a resource piece on "white supremacy culture," authored by Tema Okun. The piece identifies a set of points on the "Characteristics of White Supremacy Culture," which include features such as defensiveness, single-mindedness, individualism, perfectionism and objectivity. Objectivity implies: "the belief that there is such a thing as being objective... requiring people to think in a linear fashion and ignoring or invalidating those who think in other ways... impatience with any thinking that does not appear logical to those with power." The resolution to this problem is given as:

> Realize that everybody has a world view and that everybody's world view affects the way they understand things; realize this means you too; push yourself to sit with discomfort when people are expressing themselves in

ways which are not familiar to you; assume that everybody has a valid point and your job is to understand what that point is. (Okun Okun, n.d.)

Similar sentiments are expressed by DiAngelo with her remarks: "The belief in objectivity, coupled with positioning white people as outside of culture (and thus the norm for humanity), allows whites to view themselves as universal humans who can represent all of human experience" (59). As objectivity's Other, and where the ruse of objectivity is exposed as privilege, the particular attains a certain inverse authority: as battered and bruised knowledge, standpoint epistemology knows the world as a brutal one, not through some tweed-suited act of logical induction but through the examination of its own body. For this reason, subaltern knowing expresses an inexhaustible imperviousness to criticism: in a brutal world, any difference of opinion is a brutal difference. Even those opinions that only extend an appeal to reason demonstrate such brutality, and in so doing, confirm the very assumptions that validate subaltern authority itself. By this token, subaltern knowledge, and the regimes of government it enacts, are, like allegations of unconscious sexual repression, almost impossible to deny, and thus display an ineluctable porousness. They represent a way of knowing readily transposable across a variety of settings, easily nested together with all those other directives through which people are told what to do, how to behave, how to relate to others and ultimately how to judge and how to set about the work of maintaining and transforming themselves. There is no way to question its spread, or to propose any limits in language that does not wind up confirming its founding assumptions, redoubling its license and demonstrating the need for its further extension. In settings as varied as education, business, correction, policing, government, medicine, military and finance, the effect of this subaltern voice is unavoidable. Consider for example the case of *Antiracist Baby*, a boardbook for children aimed at readers as young as three years old authored by Abram X. Kendi, which provides nine accessible steps that a baby might go through in pursuing an anti-racist upbringing: "Antiracist baby is bred not born, Antiracist Baby is raised to make society transform" (Kendi, 2020). To suggest that children of that age are not old enough to comprehend the need to challenge racism is only to demonstrate the ubiquity of this racism itself, and of the need to press forward.

We are, with the omniscience and porousness of the subaltern, squarely at the center of the new racial sensibility's penchant for the therapeutic, where the subaltern's judgment assumes a certain therapeutic function:

what the subaltern knows becomes a tonic for white ill-health (though it is a tonic which comes with a qualifying bitter taste), and it is imperative upon white people to seek out this knowledge as a step toward the cure of the very inner racial condition from which they suffer. The value of this knowledge lies not in its falsifiable content, but in the rehabilitative effects it brings to those who enact it. This is knowledge we "need to listen to" or to "sit uncomfortably with." In this way, and much like therapeutic knowledge, subaltern knowing is almost impossible to contest without seeming to reverse it curative effects, bringing harm, and as such proves itself infinitely adaptable to a range of functions. Just as there is no institutional arrangement that cannot be made therapeutic, so there are none that ultimately resist the effects of subaltern governmentality. Both are uncontestable, owing to the nature of the claims they assert. Freud captures this valorization of therapeutic authority in his discussion of the "analytic pact" that constitutes the therapeutic relationship: "[the therapist's] knowledge is to make up for [the patient's] ignorance and give his ego back its mastery over lost provinces of his mental life" (Freud, 1940, p. 50). The therapist is, as Jacques Lacan put it, the subject "supposed to know," the one whose enlightened outlook structures the therapeutic project for a client who places complete trust in the superior knowledge of the therapist (Lacan, 1998). Against the backdrop of this omniscience, any objections raised by the analysand are easily reducible to a callow defensiveness, to the evasive maneuver of denial, thereby redoubling the urgency of the therapeutic effort itself.

Indeed, the theme of denial and related notions of resistance and defense, in both psychoanalysis and in the more mainstream therapeutic models that would replace it, also operate effectively within subaltern governmentally and the new racial sensibility. Through the lens of denial, it is thought, any reluctance on the part of the patient to participate in the analytic exchange is captured as an evasion, a resistance or a motivated hostility, easily confirmed as such within the discourse of the analytic project itself. The charge that one is in denial assumes a certain circularity: the very evasion of the charge is interpreted as an affirmation of the premise of treatment itself, a circularity for Alfred North Whitehead characterized as "a prophecy which procures its own fulfillment," or as Freud put it: "Heads I win, tails you lose" (Whitehead, 1933, p. 42). In a 2018 opinion piece in the *New York Times*, "The Heartbeat of Racism is Denial," Kendi summarizes American racism under the broad mantle of denial: "When our reality is too ugly, we deny reality. It is too painful to look at. Reality is too hard to accept." Kendi points out how this denial runs to the heart of American foreign policy under the overt racism of President Donald Trump, but also operates within the more insidious racism of liberal anti-racists, whose denial is perhaps the most toxic: "Only racists say they are not racist. Only the racist lives by the heartbeat of denial. The antiracist lives by the opposite heartbeat, one that rarely and irregularly sounds in America—the heartbeat of confession" (Kendi, 2018).

Which brings us again to the subjectifying cycle of the dispositif. It is through the capture imposed by the new subaltern governmentality that subjection, becoming subject, as the derivation of a certain traumatic self-encounter that excites and mobilizes forces, is remade as subject-to, as a normalizing process, regulated by another. The shock of a traumatic encounter with oneself, which excites a sporadic if painful inventiveness in relation to the Other, is made to confess its denials, to disclose from an interior space to an Other presumed to know, thereby assuming the form of a certain transaction, a recompense for harms done. Any development deriving from the experience of self-estrangement, any surprises or mutations that might emerge from that subjectivity or any aleatory events that might activate new relations are assessed as delinquent payments, subsumed under the logic of the dispositif's capture. Recalling Foucault's words on the double meaning of subjection, we discover this element of fixity assuming a key function for a subject that is, as Foucault puts it: "tied to his own identity by a conscience of self-knowledge" (331). Capture, in this sense, occurs as an ontology of shame is reexperienced as a jurisprudence of guilt, together with an ongoing imperative to turn guilt into good works, though with the admonition that such work should never end. Such are the effects of the new racial sensibility: an arrangement which demands of the subject that she disclose from an inner space, that she admit to what she is and has always been, that she remain pinned, tied to her own identity. And what is conserved, or captured, in this pinning is not just the white racial subject but ultimately, and by an indirect channel, an important relation within the racial order itself. Through the sovereign subaltern, transposed onto a governmentality of white racial inwardness, the broader discourse of the new racial sensibility becomes resonant with a constellation of governmental practices and authorities embedded across the texture of contemporary life.

Given the wide appropriation of these modes of knowing and judging across such a range of professional, public and private settings, given the multiple and subtle methods by which these sensibilities have been made to operate, settling into the everyday self-assessments and modes of self-monitoring practiced in everyday life, I believe it is not unreasonable to speak of the need to engage and study the emergent effects of what can be termed subaltern governmentalities, and the modes of white interiority through which they operate. And with the naming of this new regime of interiority, it is important to begin the careful and difficult work of considering how its effects, or certain of its effects, should be rethought as part of a broader politics of anti-racism.

References

Ahmed, S. (2004). Declarations of Whiteness: The Non-Performativity of Anti-Racism Borderlands, 3: 2. http://www.borderlands.net.au/vol3no2_2004/ahmed_declarations.htm

Bailey, A. (2007). Strategic Ignorance. In S. Sullivan & N. Tuana (Eds.), *Race and Epistemologies of Ignorance*. SUNY Press.

Baldwin, J. (1985). White Man's Guilt. In *The Price of the Ticket Collected Nonfiction 1948–1985*. Saint Martin's Press.

Benedict, R. (2005). *Chrysanthemum and the Sword: Patterns of Japanese Culture*. Houghton Mifflin.

Brooks, D. (2015, July 17). Listening to Ta-Nehisi Coates While White. *New York Times*. Retrieved June 12 2023 From: https://www.nytimes.com/2015/07/17/opinion/listening-to-ta-nehisi-coates-while-white.html

CIA Recruitment Video. (2021). Retrieved June 12 2023 From: https://www.youtube.com/watch?v=PHckeZoYx04

Coates, T.-N. (2015). *Between the World and Me*. Speigel & Grau.

Conrad, P., & Schneider, J. (1992). *Deviance and Medicalization: From Badness to Sickness*. Temple University Press.

Cultural Somatics Training Institute. (2022). Somatic Abolitionism is an Embodied Way of Living, Learning and Being. Retrieved June 12 2023, from: culturalsomaticsinstitute.com

DiAngelo, R. (2018). *White Fragility: Why It's So Hard For White People To Talk About Racism*. Beacon Press.

Door, P. (2020, February 3). Why Liberal White Women Pay a Lot of Money to Learn Over Dinner How They're Racist. *The Guardian*. Retrieved June 12 2023, from: https://www.theguardian.com/world/2020/feb/03/race-to-dinner-party-racism-women

Fischer, M. (2021, May 27). Guilty Parties: Two Entrepreneurs Have Built a Business Dredging Up White Women's Shame. *The Cut*. Retrieved June 12 2023, from: https://www.thecut.com/2021/05/eavesdropping-on-race2dinners-anti-racist-dinner-parties.html

Freud, S. (1940). *An Outline of Psychoanalysis* (J. Strachey, Trans. & Ed). Norton.
Freud, S. (1955). *The Interpretation of Dreams* (J. Strachey, Trans.). Basic Books.
Freud, S. (1960). *The Ego and the Id* (J. Riviere, Trans., and J. Strachey, Revd & Ed.). Norton.
Hartsock, N. (2004). The Feminist Standpoint: Developing the Ground for a Specifically Feminist Historical Materialism. In S. Harding & M. B. Hintikka (Eds.), *The Feminist Standpoint Theory Reader: Intellectual and Political Controversies* (pp. 35–54). Routledge.
Henderson, C. (2019). Rosanna Arquette Slammed for Saying She 'Feels So Much Shame' over Being White, Privileged. *USA Today.* Retrieved June 12 2023, from https://www.usatoday.com/story/entertainment/celebrities/2019/08/08/rosanna-arquette-feels-so-much-shame-over-being-white-privileged/1962475001/
Hoffman, M. L. (2000). *Empathy and Moral Development: Implications for Caring and Justice.* Cambridge University Press.
Kendi, A. X. (2020). *Anti-Racist Baby.* Penguin/Kokila.
Kendi, I. X. (2018, January 13). The Heartbeat of Racism is Denial. *New York Times.* Retrieved June 12 2023, from https://www.nytimes.com/2018/01/13/opinion/sunday/heartbeat-of-racism-denial.html
Klein, M. (1946). Notes on some Schizoid Mechanisms. *International Journal of Psychoanalysis, 26,* 99–110.
Kovel, J. (1984). *White Racism: A Psychohistory.* Columbia University Press.
Lacan, J. (1998). *The Four Fundamental Concepts of Psychoanalysis* (The Seminar of Jacques Lacan, Book XI) (A. Sheridan, Ed., and J. A. Miller, Trans.). Norton & Company.
Lewis, H. B. (1971a, Fall). Shame and Guilt in Neurosis. *Psychoanalytic Review, 58*(3), 19–38.
Lewis, H. B. (1971b). *Shame and Guilt in Neurosis.* International Universities Press.
Menakem, R. (2017). *My Grandmother's Hands: Racialized Trauma and the Pathway to Mending our Hearts and Bodies.* Central Recovery Press.
Milazzo, M. (2017, August). On White Ignorance, White Shame, and Other Pitfalls in Critical Philosophy of Race. *Journal of Applied Philosophy, 34*(4), 557–572.
Morris, H. (1976). *On Guilt and Innocence: Essays in Legal Philosophy and Moral Psychology.* University of California Press.
Okun, T. (n.d.). White Supremacy Culture. Retrieved June 12 2023 from https://www.dismantlingracism.org/uploads/4/3/5/7/43579015/okun_-_white_sup_culture.pdf
Parsons, T. (1951). *The Social System.* The Free Press.
Race2dinner. (2021). Our Programs. Retrieved June 12 2023, from https://www.race2dinner.com/our-programs

Rich, A. (1979). Disloyal to Civilization: Feminism, Racism, Gynephobia. In O. Lies (Ed.), *Secrets, and Silence: Selected Prose 1966–1978*. W.W. Norton.
Rothenberg, P. S. (2004). *White Privilege: Essential Readings on the Other Side of Racism* (2nd ed.). Worth Publishers.
Scheff, T. (1987). The Shame-rage Spiral: A Case Study of an Interminable Quarrel. In H. B. Lewis (Ed.), *The Role of Shame in Symptom Formation* (pp. 109–149). Erlbaum.
Scheff, T. (1994). *Bloody Revenge: Emotions, Nationalism and War*. iUniverse.
Scheff, T., & Retzinger, S. (2001). Shame as the Master Emotion of Everyday Life. *Journal of Mundane Behavior, 1*(3), 303–324.
Shotwell, A. (2011). *Knowing Otherwise: Race, Gender and Implicit Understanding*. Pennsylvania State University Press.
Spivak, G. C. (1988). Can the Subaltern Speak? In C. Nelson & L. Grossberg (Eds.), *Marxism and the Interpretation of Culture*. University of Illinois Press.
Sullivan, S. (2006). *Revealing Whiteness: The Unconscious Habits of Racial Privilege*. Indiana University Press.
Sullivan, S., & Tuana, N. (Eds.). (2007). *Race and Epistemologies of Ignorance*. SUNY Press.
Tangney, J. P., & Dearing, R. L. (2002). *Shame and Guilt*. Guilford Press.
Vice, S. (2010, Fall). How Do I Live In This Strange Place. *Journal of Social Philosophy, 41*(3), 323–342.
Whitehead, A. N. (1933). *Adventures of Ideas*. Free Press.
Wida, E. C. (2020, July 1). White Women are Paying Thousands of Dollars to Confront Their Racist Beliefs Over Dinner. *Today*. Retrieved June 12 2023, from https://www.today.com/food/organization-aims-dismantle-racism-over-dinner-t185504

CHAPTER 5

Beyond the Confessing Animal

Abstract A summary of the wider aims of this project considers the kind of claims that might be made for an anti-racist project. Comparisons are made with other critical engagements with white subjectivity, and questions are raised about the limits and parameters of what we might describe as anti-racism.

Keywords Anti-racism • Whiteness • Race traitor • Ambivalence

This discussion has attempted to trace pedagogies of racial inwardness across a plurality of institutional settings variously shaped by the new racial sensibility. Attention has been paid to a unique rhetorical form that exerts a double effect, simultaneously moving white readers to shame while stirring a yearning for guilt. These pedagogies induce white readers to encounter themselves in a moment of startle, prompting panic and productivity through a spasm of self-abandonment, while at the same time absorbing and containing this productivity in a system of moral equivalencies and responsibilities, psychological diagnoses and purported cures that together map this encounter onto a space of interiority. To put this differently, through the discourse of a new racial sensibility, an experience of shock, uncertainty and exposure, mobilizes a generative response that hints at a new sociability and a new subjectivity, just as this uncertainty is resolved into the rhetoric of a therapeutic program. This movement is evident across a range of texts that have been considered in this discussion.

S. Binkley, *Against White Interiority*,
https://doi.org/10.1007/978-3-031-31828-3_5

Take for example this passage from a popular work, *The Inner Work of Racial Justice: Healing Ourselves and Transforming Our Communities Through Mindfulness* by Rhonda V. Magee. An unsettling white encounter is prescribed through a set of reflective experiences such as those posed by a series of questions:

> Take a moment to check in with yourself. What was it like for you to read these words? What thoughts are coming up for you? What do you feel in your body now? What emotions do you feel as you consider what you must read? And again: where in your body are you feeling these emotions, sensing the thoughts, questions and other reactions you're noticing now? (Magee, 2019, p. 16)

These are all provocative and inviting prompts which doubtless bring upsetting and illuminating uncertainties, although, at the same time, the uncertainties and reflections they stir are quickly absorbed into a program that combines expert detachment with the narrative of a certain healing, implying the curative aim of a therapeutic operation. Consider this selection from an edition titled the *Racial Healing Handbook*, edited by Anneliese Singh and published in 2019 by New Harbinger Press:

> Healing means you begin to unlearn the stereotypical racial message you internalized about your own race and the race of others. It means you as an individual learn to recognize the wounds that racism creates in you, whether you are White or a person of color and whether you are conscious of those nicks and tears to your psyche or not. (Singh, 2019, p. 12)

Uncertainty vanishes into a "healing" process, consumed by a white interiority whose clarity is as fixed and self-evident as the very distinction between sickness and health from which it draws. Later in this same volume, in a section titled "Reclaim Your Whole Racial Self," the author continues to narrate her reader's therapeutic trajectory:

> [In previous chapters] you've noticed that a deep exploration of your race helps you understand yourself more in everyday situations related to race. You've thought about who you thought you were in terms of your race, and you've uncovered racialized stereotypes and attitudes you may have internalized. As you have done this, you've had to consider who you *really are* and want to be in terms of your racial identity. (149)

The pragmatics of healing absorbs the shocks of self-estrangement, capturing a disturbing self-awareness and a jarring abandonment in a healthier understanding, a voyage of discovery in search of who we "really are." What readers here are investing is not, as it may seem, a process of self-examination from which unexpected discoveries might develop. The ends of an inquiry into white interiority are given in advance as shame's panic is resolved into guilt's purposes.

Much has been made in this discussion of the ambiguous character of this process, and of the multiple effects of the apparatus that works to enable it. The new racial sensibility which exhorts its white readers to look within, does so in such a way as to produce contradictory effects: on the one hand it contributes to the revision of those habits upon which racial sociability depends, suggesting new ways of acting, speaking and performing before others. There are things white people no longer do after George Floyd and #blacklivesmatter, words that are not used and assumptions that are not made. This revision makes possible a public life in which some of the sting of racial sociability is tempered and in which security and respect is more readily afforded, particularly for those for whom insecurity has long been the norm. Moreover, the new racial sensibility has the broader effect of coordinating the actions of activists and managers, planners and presidents around important structural inequalities. As a consequence of protest voices associated with this new sensibility, policies are reformed, budgets are revised and perceptions are changed in ways that deliver specific and concrete results. This discussion has asked readers to look favorably on the new racial sensibility for its effect in interrogating the implicitly racial character of contemporary social life and for fostering institutional cultures and structural reforms in which the dignity of others is more readily regarded. Yet this discussion has also asked readers to consider how such interrogations, deriving as they do from managerial and therapeutic technologies designed more to regulate than to transform subjectivities, work more to reproduce institutional stability than to enact new social possibilities. As such, they contain within themselves tiny operations that work to undermine but also to reproduce those structural inequalities from which this insecurity results, enveloping white subjectivities in what has been termed a managerial equilibrium. I have asked the reader to be critical of the new racial sensibility for the way it produces new egalitarian protocols while at the same time sustaining those modes of white subjection which make these protocols necessary. In particular, I have asked the reader to be critical of the ways in which modes of white interiority are accomplished through the deployment of a certain white racial optic, a mode of Othering that is itself derived from the most classical formations of white racism, although in this case the terms of this alterity are reversed: where in an earlier time the racial Other was distained as morally abject, today the Other is venerated for its moral and epistemic distinctions. This is an optic that, while productive in many ways, ultimately produces the Other that it needs for a certain operation of white racial subjection. This is an Other made to bear a static, if paranoid gaze, a function of judgment and transparency capable of speaking the truth of a white secret, of seeing through into a great white interiority, and of bestowing responsibilities upon a guilty white actor. This Other is enshrined as a therapeutic authority who knows one's foibles better that one does oneself, but also a judge, the bearer of a fixed and heavily invested epistemic lens through which whiteness imagines itself exposed and measured, called out and unsettled, but also indebted and diagnosed, through this debt, set on a path to maturity and to the restoration of psychic health. It is an Other before whom whiteness, through a discovery of its inner life, becomes interminably guilty, though also in a sense redeemed. By calling attention to the ways in which, through this optic, white subjection is sustained through a permanent and ongoing process of self-interrogation, I have asked readers to be thoughtful of how those latent managerial operations inscribe a certain perpetuity onto the labor of white introspection, and how this perpetuity functions in sustaining a unique racial equilibrium. The excavation of white interiority, as the scene of an indelible secret, it has been argued, defines that event through which a subject gains a certain relation to herself, becoming subject, while at the same time placing that relation within the constraints of an external order with which it is sustained as subject-to.

No doubt all of this will sit uncomfortably with some readers, and with the historical moment within which it emerges. For the new racial sensibility to be both good for public culture while bad for private life (and hence, through some indirect channel, bad again for public culture), it must be viewed through the lens of an ambivalence that is not of this time. This ambivalence, I have argued, is possible if one considers the extent to which the therapeutic preoccupation of the new racial sensibility has colonized practices of white racialization, folding their ambiguities into the certainties of a totalizing moral project expressed as a therapeutic cure. In trying to take the side of this indeterminacy and uncertainty against the conviction of a certain racial pedagogy, this book has sought to recognize the necessity and value that such pedagogy brings, while it has strained to protect a shame that I argue to be ubiquitous to this moment. I have tried to do this without overpromising on the potential of this shame, and while refraining from positing white shame as itself and end, or as the basis of an alternative, consistent and programmatic anti-racism. Being ashamed, or recognizing one's shame, is not enough to extricate oneself from those structures that define the American racial order. A fully developed anti-racist program would require commitments and convictions that can only be derived from the assumption of responsibility and guilt, such as those commitments one draws from the new racial sensibility itself. While the elaboration of such a program is not the aim of this book, it is nonetheless argued that shame composes an indispensable part of what that program requires if it is to amount to more than a set of public postures and dogmatic procedures, or what I have characterized as hollowed out civilities. Some measure of responsibility, expressed in the affect of guilt where guilt implies the general assumption of a debt relation, is indispensable to a politics of white anti-racism of any sort. But so is shame indispensable to a politics that seeks to exceed the pure formality of a dogmatic calling, where shame indicates a productive and dynamic renewal not only of one's own subjection, but of the social space that ties the subject to the Other. Shame points us to a lively and open social field shared with a figure who is not reduced to the function of an all-seeing therapeutic omniscience. Shame's dynamism opens a critical and uncertain encounter that co-extends the uncertainty, inventiveness and porousness that constitutes social life itself, and for this reason plays some part in an anti-racist ethics of subjection that escapes the indurate effects of a therapeutic pedagogy.

The present discussion might be read productively alongside other appeals to an anti-racist reconstruction of whiteness which, I have argued, have a long history in anti-racist discourses. One such call came in an editorial statement introducing a journal, *Race Traitor*, authored by Noel Ignatiev and his colleagues (Ignatiev & Garvey, 1996). Launched in 1993, the journal called upon its readers to "abolish the white race," through the immediate withholding of consent to one's membership within whiteness itself. Citing John Brown's uprising at Harper's Ferry as a model of white resistance to racism, the editors invited white readers to become race traitors, engaging sovereign acts of betrayal to the implicit agreements and identifications of the racial order.

> The moments when the routine assumptions of race break down are the seismic promise that somewhere in the tectonic flow a new fault is building

> up pressure, a new Harpers Ferry is being prepared. Its nature and timing cannot be predicted, but of its coming we have no doubt. When it comes, it will set off a series of tremors that will lead to the disintegration of the white race. (Ignatiev & Garvey, 1996)

"Disintegration" is a provocative phrase, suggesting the end of a certain formation of white subjectivity, although such a program, critics contend, leaves much to be explained. Praiseworthy as *Race Traitor*'s radical rhetoric may be, it makes unreflective assumptions about the relation of white subjects to this legacy of privilege and habit, while it relies on a purely decisionistic appeal to white treasonous conduct. Calls to do white subjectivity differently, or to undo it entirely, would have to consider, its critics allege, more than a sovereign choice to betray white racial subjectivity, but the more demanding work of separating oneself from deeply engrained habits of white racial membership. I would agree with this criticism, although I would add two important points. First, the disintegration of whiteness, to the extent that it derives its purpose and project entirely from an Other to whom it responds in a relation of debt, is anti-racism that is compelled to repeat itself, leaving core elements of whiteness unexamined and unchanged. Second, a fully developed program of white treason must provide, not just the basis for a decision to break with and disintegrate an inherited white racism and its privileges, but the capacity to imagine and to produce something new to replace it, a new mode of white racial being that operates beyond existing forms of whiteness. Terminating existing modes of whiteness is no doubt important, particularly where it mean severing ties with ongoing and naturalized structures of racial domination. But an equally important challenge comes with the task of imagining and enacting new racial subjectivities to replace them—a task that cannot be accomplished for another, through the Other's eyes or in a relation of guilt to the Other, in the sense that the new racial sensibility imagines. The suffusion of shame within processes of white racial subjection indicates the extent to which the work of white racial treason, as a disintegrative but also as a productive project, is already partially accomplished, and the affective content of such a generative response is already apparent. To put this differently: an anti-racist program that exhausts itself with the elimination, suppression or critique of existing modes of whiteness has ignored the important challenge of figuring out what comes next, of creating new modes of white racial being to replace the old, which necessarily entails a productive break from the regulating gaze of the Other.

Such an objective is not as remote, or as decisionistic as it may seem. The point presented here is that, in fact, white loyalty was never so completely cemented, just as the abolition of this white race is never so dependent on a heroic white intentionality as *Race Traitor*'s critics make it seem. Indeed, the "call out" of the race traitor whose treason can be unmasked, and whose disintegration can always be recuperated in the incomplete work of a white interiority that always has one more secret to betray, serves precisely the managerial function that has been the object of this book. Subjection, Foucault tells us, always contains some possibilities that outstrip the apparatus of capture. Subjection is always an incomplete and partial process, always prone to reversals and transformations. The petulant Christian of one era becomes the flagellant of another, just as the homosexual becomes the queer, the madman the mystic poet. Subjection can always be made generative, though I have cast this process as one involving shame affects, which must be disentangled from the psychologizing guilt apparatus that encircles and confines them. In other words, white disloyalty, as I have attempted to describe it, is already present in the abundance of shame feelings and in the inevitable shame relations that characterize white racial subjection today, and which the new racial sensibility attempts to mask or transmute into its institutional forms.

Emotions are not simple instruments that can be applied to the realization of political goals, and exhortations to feel this or that in the service of a certain project misunderstand the nature of affect more generally. Yet, a certain critical attitude toward white emotionality suggests itself: disentangling shame from guilt implies a refusal, or a disloyalty not just to the strictures of white racial subjection, but to the therapeutic regimes of the new racial sensibility, whose effect is, after all, a kind of loyalty to whiteness itself, if only through labor and trauma. This disloyalty begins with the assumption of a certain skepticism regarding therapeutic authority itself—a skepticism that has long endured in the politics of the American left. Beginning early in the 1960s, against the backdrop of the institutionalization of Freudian thought in the United States, this skepticism, directed at the most basic assumptions of the therapeutic ethos, began to turn up in a variety of left critiques ranging from the intellectual histories of Lionell Trilling and the sociology of Richard Sennett to the psychoanalytic pronouncements of Phillip Rieff and the political commentary of Christopher Lasch, not to mention the philosophy of Gilles Deleuze and Félix Guattari, all of whom variously tie the therapeutic to processes of capitalist development and the impoverishment of public life and mass-based political movements (Deleuze & Guattari, 1977; Sennett, 1976; Rieff, 1966; Lasch, 1979; Trilling, 1972). For these authors, what I have termed therapeutic reason represents an extension of a capitalist managerial rationality whose function is to sustain a certain systemic form. As Robert Bellah and his associates noted in their study of American individualism almost 40 years ago, the therapeutic, which weds managerial and expressive traits "extend[s] the calculating managerial style into intimacy, home, and community, areas of life formerly governed by the norms of a moral ecology," thus displaying a "readiness to treat normative commitments as so many alternative strategies of self-fulfillment" (Bellah et al., 1985, p. 148). This skepticism continues today in the sociology of Eva Illouz and in the polemics of Frank Furedi, not to mention in the influential Foucauldian thread defined by Nikolas Rose and others (Illouz, 2008; Furedi, 2003; Rose, 1990, 1999).

Where therapeutic reason undertakes the management of our moral capacities, it does so under the sign of a restorative, psychological cure, and the consignment of what are intrinsically social affects to a remote, psychological interiority. Such an ethos blends judgment of moral culpability with the diagnosis of psychic illness. Sickness and badness combine in the figure of a moral illness that has to be understood, exposed and healed—or a debt that has to be paid. Such healing, it has been argued, transmutes shame into guilt, thus suppressing shame's effects and constraining its movement. Employing the medical rationality implied by a therapeutic technique, this rationality dislodges personal behaviors, relationships and life predicaments from their embeddedness in dynamic and shifting social fields, while valorizing the disclosure of private feeling for its effect in the healing of the actor's psychic state. In his treatment of the repressive hypothesis, which has provided a guiding thread in this discussion, Foucault implicates the therapeutic in a tradition of speech centered around the problem of sexuality. Therapeutic disclosure, favored by man "the confessing animal," as Foucault put it, derives a certain authority from the very willingness of speakers to confront and surmount prohibitions which have been placed in the way of such speech in the name of a restoration of psychic health. Confessional speech is speech in which "truth is corroborated by the obstacles and resistances it has had to surmount in order to be formulated.... in which the expression alone, independently of its external consequences, produces intrinsic modification in the person who articulates it" (Foucault, 1984, p. 162). As such, the therapeutic ethos solicits, but also subsumes the shame placed on the public disclosure of personal affects, and in so doing suppresses or masks the shame feelings that, through their inventiveness, reflect and embed the subject in dynamic relations with others. Although Foucault never spoke directly of shame, it is clear that, in this way, confessional speech implies a certain mediation of shame affect: through the therapeutic, shame is induced through difficult questions (tell us about your history of alcoholism, about your adultery, about your depression…), but at the same time shame is transcended and incorporated as an instrument of the medical operation, a necessary price to pay in the service of a valued objective, and in a sense concealed, muzzled, in a confessional discourse shielded from social affect itself. The confessing animal is already lauded for its painful self-exposure, and thus can feel no shame, buttressed as it is on all sides by a therapeutic expertise that congratulates the shameful disclosure as a necessary payment on an overdue account, a step on the road to guilt.

Through such a therapeutic reason, shame is withdrawn from the social field, prevented from doing its work. It is rendered unable to invest its productivity in its relations with others, and thus to activate a relation in which selfhood might emerge as strange, and potentially new. To undergo white racial subjection differently requires a real being-together with the Other's racial being and the Other's racial suffering, not a projection of the Other as a therapeutic mirror, but a productive engagement with the Other as an open-ended social reality. But it also requires a struggle with shame itself, and a willingness to confront the risk of shame without guarantees. When that struggle is already won in advance, as it is under the therapeutic protocol, shame's power to produce the subject differently is diminished. Thus, an anti-racist politics of white subjection would do well to greet this new racial sensibility with some ambivalence, affirming its public function while avoiding its subjectifying effects, if for no other reason than to hang on to shame and to the dynamism that it makes possible, to keep shame from this transmutation and to open up its possibilities, for this shame is the only thing that embeds us socially in a truly anti-racist, creative and generative relation to the Other. Such a program is one that recognizes the need to disentangle white subjection from processes of therapeutic reason, particularly as they are manifest in the present situation. Social being is shameful, and every historical configuration affords the shames it needs in order that subjections might occur in certain ways, variously induced and constrained, formed for the purposes of given regimes of subject-making. However, these shames are always unstable, always subject to mutation, overflowing their boundaries, and thus always defined as what Foucault termed the "odd term" in relations of power, prone to an inventiveness that escapes the program of any given dispositif (Foucault, 1984, p. 196).

In other words, the shape of shame changes with shifting social and historical dynamics, with the emergence of new technologies and new discourses on subjection. The shames that are possible today, and the shames that a new racial configuration induces, should not be drawn so thoughtlessly into public view, marshalled as payments on our guilt or surrendered so faithfully to the racial pedagogues who purport to know their truth. They should instead be explored for the disloyalties they make possible. They should be kept apart from the experts who would pin them down and pronounce on their interiorities, and instead cultivated in all their ambiguity for the generativity they might enact. Through such ambiguity, it is possible to be, I would contend, publicly guilty while privately ashamed, to be publicly responsible to a legacy of violence and inequality from which one has drawn benefits while privately, in one's own subjective relation to oneself and to others, always in a state of estrangement and disloyalty from one's own whiteness. For ultimately, such disloyalty will not remain private for long. It will inevitably, and by its own course, produce new whitenesses beyond the therapeutic script. These shameful whitenesses will, in time, shape genuinely anti-racist ways of being together with others, and ultimately undermine more than just themselves.

References

Bellah, R., Madsen, R., Sullivan, W. M., Swidler, A., & Tipson, S. M. (1985). *Habits of the Heart: Individualism and Commitment in American Life*. Harper and Row.

Deleuze, G., & Guattari, F. (1977). *Anti-Oedipus: Capitalism and Schizophrenia* (R. Hurley, M. Seem and H. R. Land, Trans.). Penguin

Foucault, M. (1984). *The History of Sexuality, Volume 1, An Introduction* (R. Hurley, Trans.). Vintage Books.

Furedi, F. (2003). *Therapy Culture: Cultivating Vulnerability in an Uncertain Age*. Routledge.

Ignatiev, N., & Garvey, J. (1996). Abolish the White Race. In *Race Traitor*. Routledge.

Illouz, E. (2008). *Saving the Modern Soul: Therapy, Emotions, and the Culture of Self-Help*. University of California Press.

Lasch, C. (1979). *The Culture of Narcissism: American Life in an Age of Diminishing Expectations*. Norton.

Magee, R. A. (2019). *The Inner Work of Racial Justice: Healing Ourselves and Transforming Our Communities Through Mindfulness.* Tarcher Perigee.
Rieff, P. (1966). *Triumph of the Therapeutic: Uses of Faith After Freud.* University of Chicago Press.
Rose, N. (1990). *Governing the Soul: The Shaping of the Private Self.* Routledge.
Rose, N. (1999). *Powers of Freedom: Reframing Political Thought.* Cambridge University Press.
Sennett, R. (1976). *The Fall of Public Man.* Norton & Company.
Singh, A. A. (2019). *The Racial Healing Handbook: Practical Activities to Help You Challenge Privilege, Confront Systemic Racism, and Engage in Collective Healing.* New Harbinger Publications.
Trilling, L. (1972). *Sincerity and Authenticity.* Harvard University Press.

Index

S. Binkley, *Against White Interiority*,
https://doi.org/10.1007/978-3-031-31828-3

GPSR Compliance
The European Union's (EU) General Product Safety Regulation (GPSR) is a set of rules that requires consumer products to be safe and our obligations to ensure this.

If you have any concerns about our products, you can contact us on

ProductSafety@springernature.com

In case Publisher is established outside the EU, the EU authorized representative is:

Springer Nature Customer Service Center GmbH
Europaplatz 3
69115 Heidelberg, Germany

www.ingramcontent.com/pod-product-compliance
Ingram Content Group UK Ltd.
Pitfield, Milton Keynes, MK11 3LW, UK
UKHW020836290926
15470UKWH00004B/1388
9783031318276